Crosscurrents / MODERN CRITIQUES

Harry T. Moore, *General Editor*

HENRIK IBSEN
The Divided
Consciousness

Charles R. Lyons

WITH A PREFACE BY

Harry T. Moore

SOUTHERN ILLINOIS UNIVERSITY PRESS
Carbondale and Edwardsville

FEFFER & SIMONS, INC.
London and Amsterdam

For Christopher

Copyright © 1972 by Southern Illinois University Press
All rights reserved
Printed in the United States of America
Designed by Andor Braun
International Standard Book Number 0–8093–0550–X
Library of Congress Catalog Card Number 71–179593

Contents

Preface

Ibsen began modern drama, amazingly enough in a time which was not an age of drama. In this he differed enormously from his great predecessors, the Athenians, the Elizabethans, and the French classicists. Most important, Ibsen opened the way for such playwrights as Strindberg, Shaw, O'Neill, Beckett, and Brecht. And although Ibsen has never really been fashionable except in Norway and Germany, his work does not die; its continuing force is both exemplary and astonishing.

In the present volume, Charles R. Lyons, the author of a volume on Brecht in the Crosscurrents/Modern Critiques series, presents some valuable new perspectives on Ibsen. He sees that dramatist's heroes in the light of a continuous dualism, forming their own concepts of realism, which reality itself opposes. This statement is a reduction to oversimplicity of what Professor Lyons works out in a highly complicated way, backing up his analyses with close references to the plays under discussion. He takes seven of these: Brand, Peer Gynt, Emperor and Galilean, The Wild Duck, Rosmersholm, The Master Builder, and When We Dead Awaken. By concentrating on a variety of plays from various phases of Ibsen's career, he is able to deal in depth with the central problems of this dramatist. And of course, he makes many references to other important plays by Ibsen, such as Ghosts and Hedda Gabler.

Because of his devotion to the subject, Dr. Lyons learned to read Norwegian, and the translations which appear in the text are his own. Mr. Lyons, Vice Chairman of the Department of Dramatic Art at University of California, Berkeley, is an experienced man of the theater whose Stanford doctoral dissertation, Shakespeare and the Ambiguity of Love's Triumph, has been published as a book. He has contributed widely to journals dealing with drama and has directed various plays by writers ranging from Shakespeare to Tennessee Williams, T. S. Eliot, and Samuel Beckett; and he has staged Ibsen's Hedda Gabler. He has also acted in many productions of such authors, which is a useful way to learn drama from the inside.

His new book on the "divided consciousness" of Ibsen's protagonists is a notable addition to Ibsen criticism.

HARRY T. MOORE

Southern Illinois University
January 4, 1972

Acknowledgments

I wish to thank *Scandinavian Studies* for permission to use material from my article on *The Master Builder* which was an early version of Chapter 6.

My translations of sections of the text of Ibsen's plays are based upon *Ibsens Samlede Verker*, Gyldendal Norsk Forlag, Oslo. These translations are literal, and they were done for this study which relies upon textual analysis. Consequently, the translations strive more for accuracy than for the grace and balance of translations designed for performance.

I would like to use this occasion to express my deep gratitude to Professor Herbert Lindenberger of Stanford University, a fine friend and invaluable colleague, whose criticism of this manuscript at various stages has been extremely helpful. The advice of two other friends and colleagues has been valuable, and I am grateful to Professors Charles C. Hampton of San Francisco State College and C. J. Gianakaris of Western Michigan University.

Introduction

Ibsen began his work as a playwright in 1849 with *Catiline* when he was twenty-one. The first sequence of dramatic works, which ranges from this initial drama to *The Pretenders* of 1863, is interesting to the student of Ibsen primarily because of the plays' sporadic movement between experimentation and eclectic imitation and, of course, in the ways in which they point toward the later plays.[1] Ibsen never stopped experimenting, but in *Brand* (1865) he produced a sharply focused exploration of the limits of human consciousness which clearly identified the ground on which he was to continue working. The plays which follow *Brand* are continuations of its subject despite the varied dramatic forms they assume.

Ibsen's work moves among obvious dramatic conventions which relate him to his time, and yet the conventional forms which he either developed or imitated are never the objective of his plays. Each technique serves Ibsen's primary purpose—the examination of the nature of consciousness. Ibsen is not primarily a realist nor a political revolutionary in any polemic sense. He uses both the detailed environment of realism and the pressures of societies in transition as means of exploring the concept of the self and its relationship to internal and external forces. Each of the heroes, from the fierce priest of *Brand* to the disillusioned sculptor of *When We Dead Awaken,* is put into a situation which reveals his divided consciousness. Each hero attempts to create a formal reality within his own imagination which will order and control the processes of experience in some conception of order, and each hero is tempted by a desire to submit to phenomenal experience without the restriction and guilt imposed by a fixed vision of reality. Ibsen's typical hero is tempted to identify his being in two opposing ways: in the creation of a concept of reality which centers upon him and affirms his being through the processes of thought and in the identification of his being through immediate sensuous experience.

Ibsen deals with the processes in which the hero attempts to create a personal vision of order which will alleviate the threat of unceasing change and the chaos of uninterpreted phenomenal events. Ibsen never defines these visions of order as reality itself. On the contrary, he insists that these structures of thought are creations of the hero's imagination. The ground of reality in Ibsen is consciousness itself. Reality external to consciousness remains equivocal in his plays, and their consistent subject is the action of the consciousness as it develops strategies to deal with that equivocation and obscurity. Each of the plays which this study discusses exposes the failure of its hero's personal concept of order, and yet each reveals the necessity of his attempt to see reality from that perspective. The plays deal with the failure and the necessity to create personal schemes of order which interpret and unify phenomenal experience. Ibsen returns again and again to the same dilemmas. These dilemmas are not ones which derive from the relationship of man and society or man and art but, on the contrary, from antithetical ways of seeing the self.

It is impossible for the consciousness to respond to the flux of phenomenal events without creating a structure which allows it to identify individual events within some notion of continuity. Myths are conceptions of order which suggest that reality is comprehensible, and the consciousness uses these schemes as if they were actual frameworks existing externally in the events which comprise experience. Ibsen explores that process, and in my discussion of the plays I use the terms *myth* and *mythical* to describe the ways in which his heroes create visions of order. Ibsen is concerned with myth, but his concern is with private processes of consciousness, not with racial or communal patterns of action.

In Ibsen's plays the process of forming ideological structures which explain and transcend the unceasing flux of perceived events is always ultimately unsuccessful. The mythical process attempts to encompass phenomenal experience but inevitably denies it. But the phenomenal base of consciousness cannot be denied. Experience cannot be held in the stasis of some ideal model, and consciousness cannot fix itself upon some unchanging idea in timeless isolation. The myth which Ibsen's heroes develop fails for precisely that reason. They cannot overcome their fascination with phenomenal experience, and the fixed myth is revealed to them as an illusionary structure whose basic function is to hold them apart from the threat of sexuality. The desire to see experience primarily as phenomenal events is voiced strongly in the plays. The "joy of life" is an insistent lure, and in the typical antithesis Ibsen repeatedly opposes the hero's messianic objective with an acute sexual temptation. The hero feels that he can only identify himself as a unique being by accomplishing an act which will order reality in some new way; and yet he also is subject to the idea that he can only experience life fully in unrestrained sexual experience. He realizes two conflicting fears: first, that it is impossible to maintain conscious control in phenomenal events in which the energies of instinct are dominant; and, second, the fear that the control and denial of those very energies destroys the very substance of experience. These fears manifest themselves throughout the plays. The fear of the loss of self-awareness within phenomenal experience reveals itself in images of fragmentation and in the frequent metaphors in which the hero sees himself surrounded by mist, the victim of a storm at sea, drowned or dissovled in the depths, falling, or being crushed. The loss of a sense of the self as independent and integral seems to create a desire to form a different kind of reality. The anxiety of Ibsen's heroes is based upon their inability to resolve the apparent antithesis between the phenomenal base of self-awareness and the ability of the mind to transcend that base in elaborate and seemingly infinite visions. Therefore this book studies seven of Ibsen's plays, beginning with *Brand*, as dramas of consciousness which probe that anxiety.

To my knowledge this book is the first attempt to read Ibsen's plays primarily as explorations of consciousness. Consequently, I have not tried to integrate the arguments of others into my own analysis. I am well aware that my own work has been influenced and informed by the specific insights of many discussions of the plays. However, the tendency of much of the best work in Ibsen criticism of the past twenty years is to relate the ideological structure of the plays to some external intellectual scheme. Despite the fact that studies which trace the influence of Kierkegaard, John Stuart Mill, and Hegel upon Ibsen do help us to locate the playwright in relation to his intellectual context and do illuminate the ideas he dramatized, the critical method of analyzing the plays as manifestations of some external scheme keeps us from seeing their own internal structure.[2] Individual readings of this type are frequently extremely revealing, but they are incomplete because they do not deal with the subtle balance between conceptions of reality held within the play, since these discussions attempt to illustrate the presence of one ideological structure.

For all practical purposes *The Quintessence of Ibsenism* has been stilled, and Ibsen the polemicist has been identified as the creation of George Bernard Shaw, who needed him for that role. The work of Ibsen criticism after the Second World War has been to affirm Ibsen the poet and to defend the plays as poetic structures which break through the conventions of their surface realism.[3] This book is certainly related to those studies, but it differs from them in a significant way. The analyses of Ibsen's metaphoric structures which attempt to see the plays as dramatic poems tend to assign fixed meanings to his primary metaphors, and the readings which result do not consider the ways in which Ibsen changes the meaning of a metaphor by shifting the context which defines it in order to reveal transitions in the hero's consciousness. The development of Ibsen's metaphors through a particular play is not merely the progressive adding on of layers of ambiguity; each of the primary metaphors is clearly transfomed at a crucial point in the action. As the following discussions will show, the central images in Ibsen's plays are not metaphoric representations of fixed aspects of reality. On the contrary, they are forms of the imagination which are used to explore conceptions of the self.

The images of Ibsen's plays seem to reveal themselves in antitheses; each major image has a counterpart, and that division of opposing metaphors suggests a strangely divided vision of human experience. Certain crucial antitheses are present in each of the plays from *Brand* to *When We Dead Awaken:* a desire for free movement within an unlimited space is opposed to a fear of restriction and enclosure; a desire for light and warmth is opposed to a fear of darkness and cold; a desire for the fixed and unchanging is opposed to a fear of movement and change; a desire for comprehension is opposed to a fear of obscurity and ignorance; a desire for a sense of the self as unique, integral, and whole is opposed to a fear of being an unspecific part of some larger, undetermined whole.

One of the most obvious recurrent images in these plays is the hero's dream that he will ascend a great height and look out upon the world. That world is sometimes conceived of as "the promised land" and always as magnificent in some way. The sense of encompassing a vision of reality within the individual mind is very strong in this image. The counterpart of this idea of a reality which can be seen and comprehended is realized in the recurrent fear expressed in the plays that the view from the heights is not a perception of "the promised land" or "all the glories of the world" but a meaningless void. In *Peer Gynt* this image occurs toward the end of the play as a sequence of ideas experienced by the hero in his moments of final despair. He uses the dream of climbing to a high mountain to see "the promised land," and then he rejects that sense of reality, declaring that he will not look because there is nothing to be seen other than wasteland and emptiness. The tension between the conception of reality as the fulfillment of promise or desire and the conception of reality as a barren waste is at the core of Ibsen's plays. This tension calls to mind the conflict between two visions of reality in Beckett's *Endgame*. Recall the image of the madman who looked out upon the "reality" of a promising and regenerative nature and saw only ashes, the void which is presented as the phenomenal reality which exists outside that strange room where the action of the play occurs.

> I once knew a madman who thought the end of the world had come. He was a painter—and engraver. I had a great fondness for him. I used to go and see him, in the asylum. I'd take him by the hand and drag him to the window. Look! There! All that rising corn! And there! Look! The sails of the herring fleet! All that loveliness! (*Pause*) He'd snatch away his hand and go back into his corner. Appalled. All he had seen was ashes.[4]

Ibsen's world is not very different from Beckett's; both share a sense that the only form which exists is a creation of the imagination, and both playwrights present their heroes suspended between an immediate apprehension of phenomena and a dream of continuity. The ambiguity of that suspended state is the primary concern of *Emperor and Galilean*, and Julian's dread is its concrete manifestation—his identification of himself as Daedalus caught in fear between the sky and the sea, "a terrifying height and an abysmal depth." Ibsen uses a spatial metaphor to reveal the divided consciousness which Julian experiences. I think that this image, which is developed in Julian's dream, is Ibsen's most clear and direct use of the metaphoric scene which he uses repeatedly.

Do you know the way in which I became filled with spiritual perception?—It happened during a night of prayer and fasting. I sensed that I was pulled far away —far away into space and out of time; for I was surrounded by full, sun-streaming day, and I stood alone on a ship with slack sails in the middle of the glassy, shining, Greek sea. Islands towered high, like pale congealed banks of clouds, far away, and the ship lay heavily as if it slept on the middle of the wind-blue plain.

Listen, this plain then became more and more transparent, lighter, thinner, until finally it was no more, and my ship hung over a terrible, empty depth. No growth, no sunlight down there—only the bottom of the sea, dead, slimy, black in all its loathsome nakedness.

But above in that infinite arch which before had seemed empty to me, there was life; there invisibility assumed form, and silence became sound.[5]

This metaphor contains the sense of a complete universe—the formlessness of the abyss matched by the form of the infinite arch of the heavens. Both the order of the heights and the chaos of the depths, however, are revealed to the imagination. In the beginning of the vision the heavens seemed empty and the sea was opaque. The identification of the formal order held in the infinite arch is a process of the imagination, and Julian does not see that form until he has seen through the transparent sea to the filth at the bottom. Even within this metaphor, the creation of the vision of the heights is initiated by repulsion at the process of the abyss.

This spatial metaphor is present in all of the plays, sometimes fragmented and strangely displaced, frequently reduced in scope under the control of plausibility, voicing itself in images of the heights and the sea, the Ice Church and the valley, the tower and the quarry.

Each extreme in this vision of the universe represents a condition of consciousness. The complexity of Ibsen's plays derives from the fact that each extreme has two faces. The achievement of that condition suggested by the image of the heights is seen in terms of light, warmth, and space—in images of infinite freedom; however, the static quality of that vision is seen as negative. The frozen form of the Ice Church in *Brand*, for example, is destructive. The demand to create a new concept of reality held in the form of the hero's private myth is a demand to stop the processes of experience itself, to withdraw into a self-contained reality. This withdrawal is a rejection of relationship because relationship reveals the dependence of the self upon external objects and persons. In this sense the created and self-contained reality is destructive. This destruction is one of the most aggressive concerns within Ibsen's plays, and it voices itself most strongly in the recurrent images of the dead who inhabit the minds of his heroes. His heroes can never free themselves from those creatures whose vitality they have denied and who are either literally dead, as Beate in *Rosmersholm*, or metaphorically dead, as Irene in *When We Dead Awaken*.

In Julian's vision the abyss shows its negative face in images of repulsion—"dead, slimy, black in all its loathsome nakedness." In its positive aspect, phenomenal experience reveals itself as "the joy of life," in unrestricted and free sexuality; in its purest form Ibsen sees phenomenal experience as the innocent play of children. The notion of selfhood can only be gained, in Ibsen's work, through fulfilling the demands of the personal myth, but those demands are presented in the metaphor of a terrifying and dangerous act. The alternative is the loss of the self—the fragmentation and incoherence of Peer's life which is seen as the consequence of his surrender to the demanding energy of sexuality. The attempt of Ibsen's heroes to discover or create *form* usually takes place in their ordering of experience in vocation; it is an acting-out of the scheme of reality. However, all of

Ibsen's heroes become disillusioned, suffering the recognition that they are the victims of internal and external energies which they cannot control. Eventually they see that their vocation has been an artifice, the embodiment of an illusion of reality, and that their own sense of identity has been the creation of a personal myth. On an external level, Ibsen's plays imitate the failure of the Christian myth, what J. Hillis Miller discusses in other nineteenth-century writers as *The Disappearance of God*.[6] Most of Ibsen's plays assume the disappearance of God, in Miller's sense, but they do not dramatize the failure of the Christian myth as a primary subject. Rather, they dramatize the failure of the mythologic process and, at the same time, affirm its necessity. The purpose of this study of selected plays from the Ibsen canon is to clarify this paradox and to reveal how it operates as a determinant of dramatic structure.

In each of the plays, the hero develops a personal myth, perhaps to fill the void left by the departure of a determining God. That personal myth is ascetic, even in the paganism of Julian's apostasy. It must be ascetic because it is mythical. As an attempt to conceive of reality mythically, the hero's search for form must deny the process of experience; the search must be for timelessness, freedom from the principle of change which is implicit within the concept of time. Ibsen's dramatizations of that movement out of time involve the hero's search for a stasis possible only in death. Myth transcends time, but in Ibsen's vision, the mythical is always vulnerable to destruction by the phenomenal and can only be permanently established in death. In the later plays, the illusory quality of that creation of form—the personal myth—is much clearer; but even in *Brand* Ibsen presents a consciousness which suffers the disillusionment of a failing mythology, and Brand's final act is an attempt to create a new fantasy.

The acute fear of formlessness in the plays is obvious: the dismembered bodies in *Brand*, the slimy abyss in *Emperor and Galilean*, the strange image of the Great

Boyg in *Peer Gynt*, the actual forests in *The Wild Duck* and the actual "depths of the sea" (in contrast to the created forms of the garret). The personal demand to realize or create form is frequently impelled by a strong desire to see oneself as innocent, to be free from guilt. The sense of guilt in Ibsen's plays is strong and seems to build upon an acute fear of sexual experience. Consequently, the assertion contained in those acts which attempt to build ideological structures that give the hero identity and continuity in society are not primarily movements toward something but movements away from that which is suggested by the image of the abyss. The mythical strategy provides only the illusion of protection from the threats of phenomenal experience. The plays consistently contain primary images of form which change into images of formlessness. The energy which is avoided becomes stronger as it is repressed, and the images of form disintegrate because they are inadequate to contain or enclose that energy. The transformation of the Ice Church into the avalanche is the prototype of that changing metaphor which destroys its own sense of form.

In reading Ibsen we grow accustomed to a particular landscape which provides a metaphoric environment for the plays. The basis of that landscape is the spatial metaphor from *Emperor and Galilean*. In its many versions, the hero deals with experience in some kind of journey, either figuratively or literally, from the dark, cramped, restricted valley to a clear, barren, uninhabited height, a place filled with the light. Balancing the heights is the omnipresent sea, a place which offers equally futile promises of freedom and comfort but which is a place of sudden and violent storms. Ibsen's landscape also includes a cold and frightening north, a place like the sea of sudden and violent storms; but this north is also the place of a primitive and destructive sexuality. Balancing the north there is the sense of a warm and vital south, a careless place of warmth and sexuality with innocence.

Ibsen's landscape is both a graphic presentation of

a sense of nature as hostile and oppressive—offering false promises of comfort and authentic threats of pain and danger—and a metaphor of consciousness itself. The ascent from the depths to the heights is, basically, a journey through the landscape of the conscious mind and the unconscious. The subject-object relationship of these metaphors is complex, and metaphoric interpretations of the plays must always build extremely carefully upon the ways in which the particular images develop within their own context. For example, the persistent metaphor of the sea in Ibsen's plays is especially powerful in its range of associations. In these plays the sea promises freedom but actually claims life rather than renewing it. It is associated with the concept of the past as unredeemable. The sea offers Ellida in *The Lady from the Sea* the illusion of a creative sexuality, but its reality is present in the image of the eyes of the dead child. In *Little Eyolf* the sea also returns the dead child whose open eyes claim his parents' guilt. The sea is the scene of the violent storm which Brand crosses to bless the man who has killed his child, the infanticide which Ibsen uses to project a sense of inherited and unredeemable guilt. Also, Brand chooses to sacrifice his own son after Gerd presents him with that appalling metaphor of the dead troll children who resurrect themselves from the depths of the sea. The sea also expresses the sense of freedom for the wild duck, and yet that bird is trapped and injured in the entangling growth at the bottom of the sea and enclosed in an artificial place which is an imitation of the depths in Hedvig's imagination. Her sacrifice takes place there in a gesture which promises freedom and expiation but which, in reality, offers neither. The sea is associated with childhood and with a dream of freedom, but that creative association is balanced with its associations of sexuality, guilt, and death. The sea is integrally involved with the sense of time in the plays, and the sea brings forth some aspect of the past which destroys the possibility of innocence in the present. In the most critical of Ibsen's antitheses, the heights which would lift Ibsen's characters from that memory are precarious and unsafe; ascending the heights inevitably ends in the fall into the depths. At the conclusion of *Brand* (which becomes the prototype of Ibsen's paradoxical endings), the image of the heights, in a fixed and comprehensible form, the Ice Church, becomes the image of the depths in the metaphor of the avalanche. Within the illusory sanctuary of the Ice Church, Brand recognizes that he is in truth in "death's abyss." *Brand* does not present the possibility of a reconciliation between phenomenal experience and the concept of consciousness which holds an image of the self as a continuous identity within a comprehensible reality. Brand's movement toward the Ice Church, which is a renunciation of phenomenal experience, is an affirmation of the vitality of his own consciousness; but that affirmation also denies the phenomenal ground of consciousness. Brand's ministry is a ministry of the self, and while that intensification of self-consciousness is necessary for him, it denies his relationship to anything apart from his own being. That denial, however, is also a denial of that aspect of his own being which would move toward another; and at the moment of his most extreme self-consciousness, that aspect of his being voices itself in a destructive release of energy.

The Ice Church is only an illusion of sanctuary; it is an attempt to contain energy within some restrictive form. The Ice Church is a version of the metaphor of the "infinite arch of heaven," that image which suggests timelessness and the resolution of process into an eternal stasis. However, that form is illusory; and the action of *Brand*—indeed, the action of each of the plays which this book discusses—is the dissolution of that image of form. The Ice Church becomes the avalanche; form becomes formlessness.

The verbal structure of Ibsen's plays always establishes an antithesis, a delicately balanced pattern of opposing metaphors, but it is impossible to interpret the plays on the basis of the values assigned that original verbal organization. Ibsen's metaphors are images of process; they are not fixed in any sense. His primary metaphors are conceptual spaces in which he can explore strategies of consciousness, in which he can pose formulations of reality. Any discussion of the plays needs to focus on an interpretation of the images as processes rather than specific identifications. These images are not symbols but metaphors in Martin Foss's sense of the distinction between symbol and metaphor:

> The simple is not the exclusion of the complex, it is the overcoming of complexity. It is never a thing but a process, it is in need of the fixed images as well as of the fixed symbols. Only in transforming symbolic fixation can the energetic process, the substantial function, the subject as fundamental drive, be recognized.[7]

In a clear sense Ibsen's heroes attempt to make certain images—the Ice Church, for example—into symbolic fixations, and those images refuse to remain static. Images of form in Ibsen's plays cannot maintain themselves because form, in his imagination, is a denial of the phenomenal ground of reality which is in constant process. The action of Ibsen's plays is the creation and dissolution of images of form. The individual readings which comprise the major part of this book analyze the dynamic process of the major metaphors which Ibsen uses recurrently, and the study explores the relationship between that constant body of images and Ibsen's experimentation with the variety of dramatic structures which hold them.

Henrik Ibsen consistently experimented in dramatic structure. His plays relate to each other in distinguishable formal groups, but even within these groups there are clear structural differences. From *A Doll's House* through *Rosmersholm* Ibsen developed a keener sense of external realism and an increasing ability to build a deep layer of surface detail which gives the illusion of realism in character. The general action is focused upon more concentrated blocks of time, and the space in which that action takes place is limited to a fully described interior which could be represented with some exactness and naturalism on the stage as Ibsen knew it. The major characters are given an increasingly dense psychological nature with pasts which explain their present condition and action. However, this movement into a form which held a surface realism is not a movement away from the concerns which direct his earlier plays. Ibsen's keen sense of observation and his perception of human detail inform his middle and later plays more thoroughly than those which come before, but the basic strategy of these plays is not the re-creation of an external reality but, on the contrary, the finer disclosure of strategies of consciousness. Ibsen's dramas are intensely subjective works, and the realistic texture which develops in his canon is primarily a means to embody the complexity of his vision of consciousness. The plays explore the nature of human consciousness relentlessly. Obviously, the conventions of realism exerted a strong demand upon Ibsen, and his plays respond to that demand. No poet is free of the conventions of his time, and his work must either affirm and exploit, or clarify and refute the vitality of those conventions. The insistence of Ibsen's central drama speaks through the conventions of his formal structure, and in the realistic plays the use of techniques of realism informs the basic drama, giving it a richness and complexity which probably no other formal structure could provide.

The realistic surface of the plays from *A Doll's House* through *Rosmersholm* works to conceal the drama of consciousness which is Ibsen's concern. But we know that such concealment and metaphoric disguise is the method by which consciousness discloses material which is either too complex or too painful for it to confront directly. The various levels of realistic detail which provide this surface texture function metaphorically, and the revelation of the processes of consciousness which Ibsen dramatizes is the work of the entire play.

Ibsen the idealist and Ibsen the realist do not vacillate. None of his works presents the concept of a reality in which the self can exist without the pain implicit in the tension of his basic paradox. The plays contain a varying balance in emphasis between mythical and phenomenal strategies of consciousness, but neither strategy is presented as an ultimate means of reconciling the self to the reality of its own being and environment. Rather the plays work to expose the impossibility of this antithesis yielding any balance between its poles in a resolving synthesis. In Ibsen, reality is incomprehensible, and the attempt to comprehend it is an attempt to enclose and contain that which cannot be held in any structure. The myth of comprehension is an illusion of being able to contain in space what cannot be restricted within spatial organization—the temporal process of phenomenal experience. However, to abandon this myth is to abandon the concept of the self, the notion of continuity, and even the concept of structure itself. To experience phenomena without a mythological formal concept is to give up the idea of the self and lose that identification in a sensual flux.

In an earlier study of the plays of Bertolt Brecht I discussed the polemic structure of his plays as a formal disguise which allows him and his spectators to accommodate the painful despair of his vision of reality by enacting a superficial pretense that this reality can be transformed into a better place.[8] The relationship between Henrik Ibsen's concept of reality and the realistic form of many of his plays is even more complex than the tension between the despair and structural polemic of Brecht's major plays. However, there is an analogy. The form of the more realistic plays seems to build upon the assumption that the nature of reality can be observed, organized, and represented in a multidetailed stage presentation. As well, these plays seem to be based on the concept that reality can be identified and imitated with some degree of clarity and can be understood within the boundaries of a formal structure. Ibsen's plays are extremely formal in their cohesive and highly concentrated sequence of events. Each event relates to the preceding event in a clear chronological sequence and develops a thematic concern efficiently and complexly. Each realistic detail contributes to a central focus, revealing and disclosing a necessary part of the ideological core. No realistic detail exists purely for the purpose of providing an interesting or merely realistic context for the action; the detail always qualifies the action in some particular way. The plays are, therefore, ordered in two significant ways. First of all, there is the external sense of order which derives from the assumption that there is a direct relationship between reality and the imitation of reality within the play. The realistic style assumes that experience can be represented within the aesthetic bounds of the play itself. Secondly, the formal integrity of the play, the clear relationship between each part and the cohesive whole, affirms the ability of the imagination to organize and comprehend the complexity of reality in a clear structure.

I am suggesting, of course, that the work of the realistic play is analogous to the mythical strategy of consciousness itself which is one aspect of Ibsen's antithetical conception of the function of consciousness. The satisfaction which we receive from our understanding of the order of Ibsen's formal structures makes the irreconcilable tension and pain of his vision of reality possible for us to confront since that comprehension of order works in a minor way, at least, to affirm the concept of order which the plays themselves deny.

Part of the difficulty with the criticism of Ibsen's plays derives from the ambiguous relationship between their formal structure and the density of their vision of reality. The plays themselves appear to be fixed and unambiguous as they work out dramatic complications with intricacy of detail, resolving the coincidences in a scrupulous and neat denouement. However, that complication and resolution is built upon a metaphoric structure which is open and dynamic. The elusive quality of reality itself, its invulnerability to containment in mythical structures, is projected through certain metaphors which transform themselves during the course of each play.

One of the most interesting aspects of the tension in Ibsen between the formal quality of his realistic plays and the vision of incomprehensible reality which they suggest is that Ibsen's realism produces the most inclusive, ambiguous, and profound versions of his central drama. The dense surface of these plays provides a complexity of perspective and a variety of levels of meaning for each of the primary metaphors; the effort to make these basic metaphors a plausible part of the formal, cohesive whole of the play enriches their content, giving them a detail they lack in the earlier plays. For example, *The Wild Duck* unmasks the mythical strategy of consciousness as illusory, and the play is relentless in its presentation of the reduced, degrading, and perverse uses of substitutes in the search which the self makes for some comprehensible vision of personal order. The following essay on this play looks closely at the image of the garret, the created imitation of the Hoidal forest, the enclosed space which substitutes for the expansive and free natural forest for the Ekdal family and also becomes, strangely, "the bottom of the sea" which traps and holds Hedvig as its victim. Here again the primary image of form is an ambiguous metaphor of sanctuary from threatening experience, and that sanctuary becomes the danger, destroying those who retreat into it. The garret is a reduced and attenuated version of the "infinite arch of heaven" in its association with the heights and its own location in the small world of the play, and this image becomes the abyss, "the bottom of the sea." That transformation manifests itself in Hedvig's identification with the wild duck and her sacrifice. The garret is another version of the image of form which becomes a metaphor of formlessness, repeating the pattern established in *Brand*.

In *Rosmersholm* Johannes's idealized relationship with Rebekka is the primary image of form, and the action of this play is the dissolution of that image. The language of this play turns again and again to the antithesis of tranquility and storm. Rosmer sees his relationship with Rebekka as peaceful, undisturbed by the frenzied energy which characterized Beate's lust for him. However, as the play proceeds, that conception of their relationship is seen to be a dream of innocence, and the latent sexuality of Rebekka's action is exposed. Their relationship proceeds toward another kind of tranquility, but that peace is the calm of injured and disabled people whose guilt makes it impossible for them to fulfill their own desires. They move toward suicide, both fascinated by the rushing water of the millrace, in an action which denies the phenomenal experience they fear but assumes the rhetoric of a sexual union. Again, the image of form resolves into an image of formlessness.

Solness's act of climbing the tower in *The Master Builder* is a version of the same metaphoric act which *Brand* contains. However, the act is given much more detail and resonance through the complexity it achieves within the relatively realistic form of *The Master Builder*. That intensification is possible in the later play because of the depth of characterization; each of the major figures perceives that act differently, qualifying and deepening our response to it. In the first place, Hilde sees the original event in Lysanger when Solness climbed the church tower as a marvelous and inspiring experience; in her adolescent imagination that act provided a means for her to transcend the prosaic nature of her own reality, giving her an objective toward which to grow. Solness's erotic encounter with her afterward deepens that experience, and in some sense she sees herself as a participant in the event. That participation is ambiguous since we learn from Solness that her active waving of a white flag during the ceremony almost caused him to fall, distracting him at his most difficult and terrifying moment. Solness conceives of that past event as the completion of an impossibility. His achievement of the impossible task freed him to confront God himself, and he sees the experience as transcendent. The event remains, however, the source of fear for him, and he is terrified at the prospect of re-creating the act. Solness's wife, Aline, denies that the event ever took place, insisting that Solness's fear of heights would make the act impossible. In their developing intimacy, Solness and Hilde create a conscious fantasy of building castles-in the air, *luftslottene;* and they discuss Solness's ascent of the tower of his newly built home as their mutual ascent to these imaginary structures. Their creative illusion is obviously an attempt to transcend the phenomenal sexuality which is the source of Solness's guilt. In Hilde's imagination his act is the manifestation of his freedom from conscience, from his fear of the ethic of retribution; and yet in Solness's imagination that act is the fulfillment of that ethic at the same time in which it attempts to free him. The event is seen in a variety of perspectives and gains a resonance from the multiplicity of interpretations which provides content for the basic paradox unavailable in the simpler structure of *Brand.*

Ibsen's movement from the expansive form of the earlier plays to the concentration of the realistic plays is, certainly, the development of his ability to frame his conflict within a restricted form which allows him to explore it more intensely. The development of the restricted and controlled but dense and profound external surface of the realistic plays culminates in the kind of abstraction in the form of *When We Dead Awaken.* Irene is the final version of the luring female who tempts and yet demands being fixed in a static innocence, and her existence in this final play provides the clear revelation that the image of form is not a renunciation of the phenomenal in any simple sense but an attempt to suspend the phenomenal in a timeless state, free of change and loss.

The following chapters are detailed analyses of the individual plays discussed briefly in this introduction. Each of the discussions is relatively independent, but their primary concern is Ibsen's exploration of the mythological function of consciousness which attempts to create an image of selfhood and his recognition of the failure of that process. These individual readings, therefore, concentrate upon the images of form which are developed in the plays and explore the processes in which these images develop, transforming themselves from dreams of order and comprehension to realizations of formlessness and obscurity. Each of Ibsen's plays from *Brand* to *When We Dead Awaken* is based upon his consistent examination of this event in consciousness. I have selected only seven of the plays in order to discuss each in close detail. *Brand, Peer Gynt,* and *Emperor and Galilean* form a foundation upon which Ibsen's later work builds. *The Wild Duck* is the culmination of the movement in Ibsen's experimentation with realism and encompasses the concerns and techniques of that sequence of plays more richly than *A Doll's House, Ghosts* or *An Enemy of the People.* The use of dense realistic detail as dramatic metaphor in *The Wild Duck* is most skillful in this play and provides the best model from this period. *Hedda Gabler* and *The Lady from the Sea* are omitted from the book, unfortunately. I particularly regret the absence of a detailed analysis of *Hedda Gabler,* but I feel that it is more important to include *Rosmersholm* because the complexity of Rebekka as an image which works to clarify the movement between the phenomenal and the mythical is a major achievement in Ibsen's work. *The Master Builder* is the most successful realization of Ibsen's basic drama, in my opinion. I include *When We Dead Awaken* in order to illustrate the ways in which Ibsen continued his experimentation through his final work. In a sense each of the plays which I have included is an experimental play, an attempt to sound the paradox more clearly. This study does emphasize the conceptual unity of Ibsen's plays, but the recognition of their integrity allows us to see the development of the formal structures which both hold and shape his exploration of the nature of consciousness.

C. R. L.

Berkeley, California
2 January 1970

Henrik Ibsen

1

Brand

Although *Brand, Peer Gynt,* and *Emperor and Galilean*
were written between 1864 and 1875, it is clear from
Ibsen's letters that all three of these extensive dramatic
narratives were actively within his imagination during
his first exile from Norway, his stay in Italy from the
spring of 1864 until the fall of 1868. These three plays
are exceedingly different in form, and yet they are closely
related in the sense that each explores the nature of the
human consciousness in conflict with those forces which
would determine its action. Although each has been
produced, these works were all written for the reader
rather than the spectator. *Peer Gynt,* of course, is the
only play of this group which has a consistent stage history. It has a vitality and imaginative freedom which
seems to demand performance. *Brand* and *Emperor and
Galilean* are difficult and unwieldy texts for performance; but the richness and density of their verbal structures demand critical attention. The honesty with which
these plays confront Ibsen's basic concerns gives them an
importance for the student of Ibsen that goes beyond
their value or reputation as theater pieces.

Ibsen traveled to Italy after receiving a grant which
gave him some freedom, although that sum had to be
supplemented with the support of friends. The scale of
these ostensibly nondramatic works might derive from
this sense of freedom, or from a disenchantment with
the pressures and limitations of the stage itself. It is

necessary to note that within this period Ibsen did write a play designed for performance, *The League of Youth* (1869). While this work is interesting, especially as it prepares for the kind of ironic realism which will voice itself in the more plausible and controlled plays to come, it does not have the depth and interest of the three lengthy dramas which consumed almost nine years of Ibsen's life.

In *Brand* Ibsen's basic themes and major metaphors are clearly at work. *Brand* is the dramatization of its hero's ascent from the darkness of the valley into the light-filled heights. However, while Ibsen has not constructed an allegory with patent and fixed associations, the density of the poem is revealed in its particular symbolic configuration, especially in the complexity of the spatial metaphor.

The description of the first scene of the play is revealing: "*High upon a snow-covered mountain plateau. The mist lies dense and oppressive; it is raining and approaching darkness.*" Initially we see Brand attempting to make an ascent up the mountain through a dense mist. The way itself is extremely hazardous. The peasant and his son who meet Brand point out the danger in proceeding through the fog. They fear that they all will fall through the crust of ice and snow to "an abyss that none can sound." Brand's first act is an attempt to climb through what is dense and obscure, following a course which threatens life itself. He chooses to continue, but the peasant and the boy turn back. The failure of the peasant is particularly significant. The two are traveling to make a final visit to his daughter who is dying. She wishes to have her father's blessing before her death. The peasant's choice of the safer course and his return home is a denial of his daughter. The act is the first in a series of parental rejections, failures, and compromises in *Brand*. Brand despises the peasant because the man is not willing to commit himself to that one dangerous act. The peasant refuses because he is unwilling to die, and he justifies his refusal on the basis of his other familial obligations. Brand's anger at the other man's choice reveals his own ethical demand that one's whole being be focused upon a particular act. This willed concentration upon a single act denies the presence of complexities and equivocations in the ethical situation. Brand himself values the sense of identity which one achieves by the embodiment of the will, the potential the peasant's act could have fulfilled. Brand moves onward through the storm.

It is important that Ibsen saw Brand's movement in this scene as a journey through and out of obscurity, a movement from darkness to light, from storm or tempest into calm. The movement into the storm is dangerous; it threatens life itself; it is opposed to the safety and security of home; and yet that use of the will offers protection from other temptations. Through the mists which are clearing, Brand sees the figures of Einar and Agnes, bathed in light. Brand identifies the lovers incorrectly as brother and sister, moving them, in his own imagination away from the threat of sexuality. They venture close to the abyss and are in danger. Brand himself warns them, but in their ecstasy, they dismiss the threat of death. The following scene with Brand, Agnes, and Einar clarifies Brand's isolation; it reveals the antithesis between Einar's romanticized concept of a benevolent and anthropomorphic deity and Brand's identification of God in action. Brand holds a vision of God as the embodiment of a spiritual energy focused in action.

> *But your God is not mine!*
> *Mine is a storm where yours is a powerless wind,*
> *Unyielding where yours is deaf,*
> *All-loving where yours is uncaring,*
> *And he is young as Hercules—*
> *Not some failing grandfather!*
> *His voice struck with lightning and terror*
> *When, as fire and thornbush, he*
> *Stood before Moses on Mount Horeb*
> *As a giant standing before a dwarf's child.*

Brand celebrates a sense of unified being, affirming either a life dedicated to the satisfaction of passion or asceticism, but above all, firmly dedicated. He sees ordinary life in images of fragmentation and diffused identity. Brand's concept of the realization of a unified being, a self which is whole and comprehensible is clear:

> *. . . from these fragments of soul,*
> *From these severed torsos of spirit,*
> *From these heads, these hands,*
> *A whole shall grow, so God shall know*
> *His man again, his greatest work*
> *His heir, Adam, young and strong.*

Einar and Agnes are about to leave the mountain village for a journey on the sea to be married. But when they leave Brand, Agnes's imagination is filled with the vital image of this exceptional man, and they both experience a sensation of cold, recognizing that their way is now shadowed and qualified by this strange encounter.

Brand's return to the place of his childhood is not a nostalgic reunion. The comfort of finding familiar objects and scenes is more than balanced by his pain at being reminded of his relationship with his mother. He sees that pain in the image of obscurity, the dimming of his vision. The intrusion of that memory is for him an oppressive burden and a nightmare:

> *There is a crushing weight upon me.*
> *It is a burden to be related to one*
> *Whose spirit is always directed toward the earth,*
> *Apart from me.*

Brand sees himself as a shorn and fettered Sampson, and in this state of consciousness he meets the figure of Gerd. Gerd is one of those charged Ibsenian figures who seem to appear at crucial moments in the life of the protagonist in order to fulfill some strange, dark function. However, while she is a complex figure in terms of the possibilities of interpretation, she is neither obscure nor obscuring. On the contrary, Gerd illuminates much that otherwise would be obscure in *Brand*. Here, Gerd poses the most obvious conflict of the poem, and Brand begins to explore the dialectic within his own imagination: the choice between an earthly ministry, tending to human needs, and the absolute commitment to an ideal. The choice is clarified in the image of two churches opposed to each other: the actual church, the small dark church of the village, and the threatening mountain cathedral, the natural structure which has been given the name Ice Church. Brand considers the conflict after Gerd leaves him:

> *That [Gerd] was also a churchgoer.*
> *In the valley—on the heights, which is best?*
> *Who takes the most wandering and confusing course,*
> *Who strays furthest from peace and home?*

Brand dedicates himself to the earth church, seeing the village as sullied, demonic, polluted, with himself as its purifier. Brand's way, in a literal sense, has been a groping through the obscurity of the fog; here his ideological way is seen as a corresponding journey through a hostile obscurity.

The most important aspect of this scene, however, is the clarification of the complexity of Gerd's motive to ascend to the Ice Church. Gerd is not merely ascending to the Ice Church; she is fleeing, running in terror from the falcon who pursues her: "He will tear me with his claws." To Gerd, the Ice Church is safety from the ever-present falcon and freedom from the foulness of the village. To Brand the Ice Church is danger.

> *Never go there; a sudden gust of wind*
> *Has often been enough to crack the glacier;*
> *A shriek, a rifle-shot, is enough—*

The ambiguous sense of the Ice Church as sanctuary and threat is crucial to our understanding of *Brand*. In one sense the Ice Church is related to the image of "the infinite arch of heaven"; it is the objective of Brand's journey, and his presence there will signify, apparently, his achievement of the perfect, willed act. However, at this point in the drama, all of the complexity of the metaphor of the Ice Church has not come into play. We do know that this place has a certain numinosity for Brand: he is attracted by it, and yet we recognize that he is fearful of it. It is a sanctuary for Gerd, a place where she is safe from the torment of the falcon and free from the sordidness of the village. We also realize that Gerd's action is irrational, perhaps lunatic; and that her conception of the Ice Church as sanctuary is a fantasy.

Eventually each of the women associated with Brand is related to the image of the falcon. Gerd, his mother, and Agnes are bound together in this strange way. The relationship seems to derive from Brand's own concept of guilt, but the way in which that sense of guilt inherited from his mother operates in the play is strange and unclear. In his discussion of the play, Brian Downs proposes that Ibsen used Kierkegaard's notion of two kinds of tragic guilt: the aesthetic which exists only for the purpose of the work of art and the ethical which is the consequence of a deliberate choice.[1] Downs suggests that the emphasis in *Brand* upon inherited guilt derives from the fact that Ibsen weighed an aesthetic guilt upon his hero to balance the ethical guilt which is the consequence of Brand's renunciation of his wife and child. In Downs's intelligent discussion, this interpretation works well. However, I think that the notion of guilt itself is integral to the basic struggle of consciousness imitated in *Brand*, and it is necessary to look closely at Ibsen's method of presenting that concept.

Brand's first exceptional act is to cross the fjord in a raging storm in order to bring peace to a dying man who killed his starving infant child in order to save the baby from suffering and then wounded himself fatally. Brand seems infused with energy when he learns of the deed, and his strength and courage attract Agnes, who makes the journey with him. These two are the only ones willing to risk their lives in the hazardous journey.

The next scene takes place after the man's death, and Brand discusses the nature of that death. The quality of his response to the event is very revealing. In his early discussion with Einar, Brand conceived of fallen man in images of dismemberment and injury. Ibsen projects Brand's rejection of human experience in violent physical metaphors. The antithesis of a clear, defined, comprehensible sense of being is seen in images of dismemberment. However, the idea of death as an integrating, unifying, resolving force informs Brand's discussion of the father's death. He speaks of death bringing "calm and light." Death in Brand's imagination is the healer of fragmentation, seen as the antithesis of images of dismemberment and suffering. There is a strong fascination with death in this play, manifested in the death of the peasant's daughter, the image of the man who kills his child, the deaths of Agnes and Alf, the death of Brand's mother, the grotesque and critical memory of Brand's dead father, and the final death of Brand and Gerd. There is hardly an idea in *Brand* which is not qualified and complicated as the play progresses, and the sense of death as a unifying and resolving force is also qualified. Immediately after Brand suggests that death itself has transfigured the identity of the father who has killed the child, he reveals his own fear that this sense of calm and light may be an illusion. Brand's attention moves to the remaining children who will bear the burden of their father's guilt:

> *But these two sat terrified,*
> *Staring with wide-opened eyes,*
>
> . . . .
> *They whose souls received a stain,*
> *Etched in, which endless washing*
> *Could neither cleanse nor wash away.*
> *Even when they are bent, silver-haired old men—*
> *They, whose course of life rises*
> *From that evil memory—*
> *They, who now shall grow in light*

From his nocturnal crime—
They can never burn out
The thought of this mortal crime.

. . . .

From them, perhaps, shall proceed
Generation to generation of sin and crime.
For what reason? The abyss answers,
"They were the sons of their father!"
What shall be destroyed in silence?
What shall gentleness smooth out?
Where does guilt begin
In our familial inheritance?

The end of this speech is important to our reading:

. . . on the brink of the abyss, dances
The crowd without mind or sense;
Souls should cry and tremble,
But no one among them sees
What towering guilt rises
From those little words: to live.

In that ecstatic speech Brand discloses one of the aspects of the image of the abyss which is the source of its terror —the function of sexuality, the human creation of man: "The abyss answers, 'They were the sons of their father!' " Ibsen's images of *form*, which are always antithetical to the sense of process, are static; and the illusions or myths of form which Ibsen's heroes attempt to establish within their own consciousness deny process. In the later plays the association of the illusions of form and the state of innocence is much clearer, but the association is undeniable, although sometimes obscure, in *Brand*. Brand's attempt to realize a fixed identity manifests itself in his attempt to free himself from both mother and child, from the generation which fathered him and from the generation which he fathered. The concentration upon the act, informed by neither past nor future, is an effort to act on the basis of a determined and freely chosen motive. The dream of acting freely, apart from the process of time, is the myth which Brand attempts to enact; but the reality of process, embodied in his own consciousness as sexual guilt, consistently affirms itself. Brand's renunciation of sensuality is an attempt to expiate his parents' sin, the way in which his sense of guilt voices itself. Brand's created myth of the will is fragile, however, and vulnerable to the persistent demands of reality. That reality forces itself upon him in the person of Agnes.

Brand is able to reject the offer of becoming the priest of the village church, seeing clearly that this limited vocation would force him to sacrifice his focused dedication to realize the divine will embodied within his own. However, Agnes provides a new vision, and Brand reforms his concept of self-fulfillment. Brand, as discussed earlier, has posed a concept of the rebirth of fallen man; but he has seen it primarily in terms of his own consciousness. Agnes ecstatically predicts that man will be re-created through Brand:

> . . . *a greater earth I see;*
>
> . . . .
>
> *And I hear voices interpret:*
> This earth *you shall people!*

Brand responds to her ecstasy in an attempt to reform his sense of mission, seeing himself and Agnes as the instruments of a regeneration of man. Until this moment nothing has been able to lure Brand from his fixed desire to embody will, and yet Agnes provides the temptation to change his vision of will. At this moment in Brand's experience Agnes is the innocent young girl who combines beauty and purity. Untouched as yet by sexual processes, her presence can promise Brand the extension of that innocence into a sexual relationship which will not bring him guilt. Brand's vision of Agnes is introduced in images of light, childhood, and play; but their relationship is affirmed in their traveling together through the storm: Gerd is there, as well, taunting them from the shore, throwing stones at them as she does at her falcon; and a woman watching them in the storm shouts: "Black as raven's wing, streams/His wet hair wildly." Agnes may present herself to Brand's consciousness as an image of innocent sexuality, but the complexity of this scene is suggestive: the association of their relationship with the sense of storm and angry sea, the image of them as Gerd's target, the direct association of Brand and the falcon itself, the infanticide, and Brand's insistence on inherited guilt or original sin. This complexity suggests that Agnes herself does not offer Brand an authentic opportunity to create a new generation, the rebirth of the earthly in some miraculous innocence. In simpler terms, Agnes does not provide Brand the freedom from guilt that he seeks in her image. She is that image for him only momentarily; immediately after defining his new mission, his recurring sense of guilt qualifies his confidence:

> *Space within the whole earth's span*
> *For becoming complete in oneself—*
> *That is a valid right of man,*
> *And I shall claim no other.*
> (After thinking in silence)
> *To become complete in onself? But with the weight*
> *Of familial inheritance and debt?*

His doubt is answered immediately by the presence of Brand's mother, that figure who is the clearest personification of guilt for Ibsen's hero. Moving within the imagery of darkness, obscurity, and guilt, she enters, hiding from the light and cursing the sun.

The concept of *parent* in *Brand* is difficult. As father, Brand himself is to sacrifice his child in order to fulfill his dream of the realization of will. In his imagination, his mother is the manifestation of all that is vile in human nature: she is greedy, lustful, and yet willing to sacrifice her lust for her greed. This woman is the most acute image of guilt in the play, and Brand regards his own suffering as the expiation of his mother's guilt. His whole sense of alienation seems to build upon a crucial incident in the past. As a young child he entered the room where his father's body had been put to await burial. Here, not realizing that his father was dead, he saw his mother come into the room, and ransack the body—searching for money. Brand's renunciation of sexuality seems to be associated with this strong revulsion at his mother's greed. Witnessing the scene, Brand moved from innocence to experience, and at this point he seems to have accepted the reality of guilt.

She grasped, she begged, she fretted, swore.
She was after a hidden track,
And she found it, immediately, with ecstatic anguish
She pursued, as a falcon seeking out his prey!

The strange associations of sexuality and death, sexuality and greed, sexuality and inherited guilt meet in this rich childhood memory. Guilt within *Brand* has to do with the realization that the self is driven or motivated by energies of greed, acquisitiveness; this image is strangely sexual and antisexual at the same time. The metaphor of the falcon is clearly a metaphor for lust, and yet the greed of Brand's mother is, in itself, a denial of sexual fulfillment—her choice of her old husband denies her love of the man who eventually fathered Gerd. The difficulty here has to do with the fact that to Brand sexuality itself cannot be divorced from the kind of imagery of festering, decay, rottenness, greed, and acquisitiveness which are part of the content of this early memory.

Brand's mother has acquired a sizeable fortune, building upon the wealth she inherited from her husband. Brand demands that she give up this wealth, offering it as a kind of sacrifice; but she consistently refuses. When Brand hears that she is dying, he refuses to go to her to give her his blessing. Even when she agrees to give up half of her wealth before she dies, he continues to refuse her, affirming that she can gain value for him only in a complete renunciation.

All that binds you now to the earth
You must willingly cast away
And walk naked toward your grave.

Brand equates her love of possessions with a mother's love for a child and puts the act of renunciation in the image of *Kindermord*: "Cast an infant into the middle of the fjord/And implore God to consecrate your deed!" Brand's refusal to comfort his dying mother marks his final denial of her, and he learns of her death at the same time that he learns of his son's illness which will prove fatal unless he is moved to a warmer climate. In this one scene, Brand renounces both mother and son. His action builds upon that concept of identity gained through a total focusing of the will:

> It *is no martyrdom to die*
> In *anguish upon a cross;*
> First will *that death upon the cross;*
> To will *through every mortal pain*
> To will *amidst the dread of the spirit,*
> That *is to gain redemption.*

Brand's course is an attempt to free himself from a relationship with anything apart from his own being. He makes an effort to enact his conception of willed action within the experience offered by Agnes, but the demanding presence of his son clarifies his dependence. Alf sickens in the cold, damp climate, and it becomes clear that his life depends upon Brand's giving up his mission and taking his family to a warmer place. Brand seems willing to give up his work to save the child, but Gerd arrives, revealing the quality of Brand's imagination by voicing his own fears. She comes into his garden in a state of ecstasy, rejoicing that the priest has given up his ministry. She declares Brand's departure will release the trolls from their bondage. Gerd defines his act as compromise, seeing it as demonic; and she identifies Agnes and the child as his idols, the objects of a false worship. Most significantly, she describes how Brand's idolatry will free the demonic energies of the abyss:

> Can you see the thousand trolls
> The country priest has sunk into the sea?

Can you see the thousand dwarfs?
Until now they lay buried
With his seal protecting them from ruptured graves.
Neither sea nor grave can hold them;
The swarming, wet, cold
Troll children, appearing dead, grin
Overturning the boulders of the avalanche.
Hear the screams: mother and father!
Men and women answer;
A country man moves among his dead
As a father among his sons;
A country woman takes her dead,
Putting it to her breast to feed;
Never before carrying herself so proudly,
Not even when she bore her child to baptism.

At this point in Brand's troubled groping toward some sense of himself as a human being, he fears the deterioration of his own ideal through his identification with Agnes and the child. Gerd becomes a projection of that fear. This image of the dead children, cold and damp from the sea and earth which contained them, is a vision of the death of Brand's own child; on the other hand it presents the way in which the concept *child* works in Brand's consciousness. *Child* is the regeneration of evil, the manifestation of some demonic process, irrational and disordered. Brand sees that the betrayal of his mission would release those terrifying energies which are contained in Gerd's image of the resurrected troll children.

After his son dies, Brand learns of the curious connection between Gerd and his mother. The mayor tells him that his mother was courted by an attractive and intelligent gypsy. When she rejected him to marry Brand's father, an old man whose money she desired, the gypsy turned to a woman of his own people; and Gerd is the child of that union. The fact of his strange relationship to this demented girl comes to Brand as one of those acutely disturbing revelations of the past which shock Ibsen's heroes. Brand sees this relationship as part of a complex pattern of expiation, and he finds this pattern obscure and confusing—again using an image which suggests his course as a groping toward an unknown objective:

> O, *expiation here is endless.*
> *So wild and so confused are the*
> *Thousand intricate webs which destiny spins—*
> *There lies sin blended with the fruit of sin,*
> *One infecting the other,*
> *And he who looks therein, sees righteousness*
> *And foulest injustice become one.*

Brand sees Gerd as the agent of his son's death, that death which is the expiation of his mother's sin. To Brand, Gerd's voice is the voice of God which came to him at the moment of choice:

> . . . *this broken soul came into being*
> *Because my mother's soul ran wild.*
> *Thus God uses sin's offspring to gain*
> *Balance and justice;*
> *Thus from the heights he hurls*
> *Affliction down upon the third generation.*

Gerd is a complex image: she is the embodiment of the mother's sin; and at the same time her retreat to the safety of the Ice Church, a movement from the darkness of the village and the threat of the falcon, parallels Brand's movement toward the Ice Church and clarifies that it is an escape, an irrational evasion of the threat of sexuality. In a strange sense, Gerd lures Brand away from the village and up the mountain toward the heights of the Ice Church; but that lure is ambivalent. She is a projection of eroticism herself, and yet she is fleeing the falcon. The falcon is the image given to Brand's mother as she violates the corpse of Brand's father, and the sense of greed, acquisitiveness, preying, and sexuality are never, in this text, far from the metaphor.

After Alf dies, Brand demands that Agnes give up all that would remind her of the dead child. Brand leads Agnes through the process of willed renunciation that he desires for himself. Agnes herself sees that process as a temptation, and she sees the image of her dead child luring her toward Heaven.

> *The sacrifice of the child, that painful sacrifice,*
> *Has carried my soul from death;*
> *He was given me only to lose;*
> *I had to be lured to victory!*

The movement of renunciation is consistently seen in the play as a lure, a temptation. Agnes realizes that this renunciation is a confrontation with Brand's God and that she cannot see God and live. The renunciation which Brand demands for both is the acceptance of death. Agnes's willingness to act inspires Brand, and he identifies her action as the source of light: "What a light you kindle!" And yet her acceptance of death is also a movement into darkness: "An oppressive mist lies over me . . . Victory took all of my strength; I am weary, I am weak. . . ."

Brand's final sacrifice is the sacrifice of the rebuilt village church, a structure purchased with the inheritance of his mother's wealth. Brand makes that sacrifice after meeting Einar once again. Einar has experienced a state of extreme desperation in which he immersed himself in sensuality; from that despair he has moved into an inflexible and frenzied renunciation of everything which is earthly. Einar sees himself as a personification of expiated sin, pure and innocent and reformed:

> *On me nothing soiled remains.*
> *I am washed by cleansing faith;*
> *Scraped clean of each splash of mud*
> *Upon the sacred's wash board.*

Brand seems to receive amazing energy from this concept of innocence, seeing this vision of man made pure as a force which can break his own restrictions. He renounces the new church to the people who have come to dedicate the sanctuary, throwing the keys of the church into the river. He sees the gesture as a sacrifice made to the abyss:

> Enter there, you slave of earth,
> Creep through the vault's crack;
> Your back is limber, creep and bend;
> Let your sigh from the sickening darkness
> Course the earth like heavy poison
> Like a powerless, dying man's grasp.

Brand's concept of church itself moves from the small sanctuary, the place of common earthly service, to the symbolic church. Knowing that the mob which starts to follow him will eventually fall away, he begins his ascent. It is important that this movement is initiated by his desire to attain the quality of innocence present with Einar's self-image. When Brand is deserted by his people, his imagination ranges over various images of fear and dream and hope, concentrating, however, upon the basic tension present in his consciousness between his acute guilt and his dream of innocence. His fears come to the surface in a frightening image of a little child wandering through a dark and shuttered room, terrified by unknown shapes which seem to shriek at him. The child is frightened within this dark and haunted space, while the day is light and warm outside. Again the primary quality of the metaphor is movement from the darkness and enclosure into light and space. Then Brand moves to the comparison of sensual human beings with the king who refused to bury his dead wife, returning to her body and loosening the linen to feed himself with the illusion that she would live again. His conception of the reality of experience returns once again to the concept of process:

> Dreams cannot give life to a corpse,
> A corpse must rot within the earth;

The only task a corpse can fulfill is
To nourish the newly germinated seed.

Brand seems to reject the notion of sacrifice at this moment, accepting his failure, seeing his renunciation of Agnes and Alf as futile, because the temptations are still present within his own consciousness.

Agnes, Alf, the shining day,
Life in peace, life in rest,
I exchanged for battle and sorrow,
Tore my breast with sacrifice—
But still did not kill mankind's monster.

Brand's effort in this play is to affirm himself with an action that identifies his consciousness with Divine Will (which he identifies as the ultimate conscious force). He desires that his consciousness contain the coincidence of the human and divine, transcending the finiteness of his experience. The nature of what we have called the mythical concerns time in a complex and difficult way in *Brand*. Mythical thinking is formal in the sense that form was defined earlier. Ibsen has used the various images related to the abyss to describe the formless world external to consciousness, the phenomenal environment in which consciousness exists. Ibsen's metaphors project a sense of that reality as a sequence of experiences unrelated, unshaped, and hostile to the self. In *Brand*, the threat of change manifests itself in a fear of process because, to Brand, process implies the implementation of energies apart from conscious control and, consequently, the destruction of the sense of the self as unique and self-determining. Ultimately, of course, the recognition of process is a recognition of change and death. The creation of a myth is an attempt to transcend the sense of fragmentation, ceaseless change, and the finiteness of experience seen only phenomenologically. The sense of myth stops the operation of time, holding the quality of a single moment in an infinite future. Form, the comprehension of reality in a single structure, attempts to see reality spatially instead of temporally.

The enactment of a myth is an attempt to transcend time; it is a movement out of time; and, as such, it is a movement toward death. Ibsen's dramatization of that movement out of time is, primarily, a movement from temporal guilt to a condition of static innocence, but that stasis is possible only in death. In some of the plays the attempt to transcend process and fix a condition of innocence takes the form of the hero sacrificing the object of his desire (or some other object which represents his desire). Frequently that strategy fails, disintegrating the hero's faith in that mythical construct; and he is forced to create a deliberate illusion of order which, when fulfilled, will take him into the stasis of death. The complex of meanings of Alf's sacrifice in *Brand* is important. On one level Brand's action, which insures the death of his son, is an attempt to halt the process of expiation which he senses working in the transmission of guilt from one generation to the next. However, that withdrawal from the processes of guilt is not made for the son, but to free himself.

In Brand's imagination, action itself is supreme. Qualifying circumstances are dismissed, and all the energies are focused in the fulfillment of the act. Brand's failure comes through his ignorance of the totality of the self, through his illusion that the conscious will is the exclusive source of action. Correspondingly, much of the difficulty with the criticism of Ibsen's work derives from the fact that it has too frequently assumed that Ibsen's basic conflicts were between the individual and forces external to him, between the individual consciousness and a repressive, arbitrary, hypocritical ethic. In most of Ibsen's plays the vilification of hypocrisy is clear; however, the restrictive ethic always manifests itself in the consciousness of the protagonist. The struggle is between aspects of the self; the conflict remains an internal one. Brand's ego manifests itself in his definition of will, the ideal of renouncing all which would qualify purely willed action; and this movement of the ego is further qualified by the demands of the totality of the self. His denial of the pressure from the unconscious is an attempt to assert the primacy of the ego or to act as if the ego were the total self. *Brand*, however, dramatizes the impossibility of that attempt; and Brand's experience within the Ice Church clarifies that impossibility. In one sense, the chasm is the objective of Brand's ascent; it is the height to which he has aspired—his presence there figures his achievement of pure will, a complete renunciation of those forces within his own being which would lead him away from a purely determined act. In this sense, the Ice Church is his achievement of a triumph over all those forces which relate to the image of the abyss, the depths of the sea, and the village that hovers at the foot of the mountains next to the sea. The depths of the sea, which bring forth the dead troll-children in that crucial image, the earth, the complex of metaphors of festering, cancer, rot, fetidness—all those images which project a revulsion at sexuality—are the antithesis of the image of the Ice Church. Of course, the relationship of Agnes and Alf to that complex of images is indirect, but the final association comes in Brand's recognition of the relationship of Agnes and the falcon. The threat which Agnes poses is the threat of sexuality, the loss of the sense of pure will in the submission to the instinctive energies of sexuality. Brand's movement toward the Ice Church and his final condition there is an escape from the erotic. Brand sees himself pursued, and his movement toward pure will qualifies that asceticism as much as the potentially ironic voice of God at the end of the play. Agnes appears as a phantom in the Ice Church because her presence is still vital within Brand's consciousness. The fear and attraction of sexuality is still strong and must be ruled out of his being. Here in the Ice Church that denial is possible, and Brand does not move toward the abyss, as Agnes tempts him, but stands firm. His struggle here is more intense, surely, than its more realistic form earlier, since the whole drama is abstracted in his dialogue with Agnes. She clarifies to Brand that his concept of willed action, of renunciation of the earthly, is a dream. She identifies Brand's concept of the will as an illusion which is impossible to maintain within the reality of experience. However, the presence of Agnes in this scene is the presence of a phantom; she herself, and that interpretation of experience which her presence figures, is a fantasy. More accurately, perhaps, the phantom reveals that which in Brand's own consciousness must be considered: the sense of reality which sees experience primarily in terms of relationship, of identification of the self as it exists in sexual experience. It is that sense of reality within his own consciousness which pursues Brand and from which he flees into the apparent sanctuary of the Ice Church. Here the image of Agnes as the threatening falcon becomes clear. She declares that her presence signals the release from his "fevered dreams." She attempts to persuade him that her death and the death of their child are not realities but rather the manifestation of his own frenzy. She brings forth the past, before the sacrifice made to Brand's will, as a time of peace; and it is that concept which breaks Brand's temptation. He cannot accept that vision of experience.

THE PHANTOM.   . . . then it was a time of peace.
BRAND.   Peace!
THE PHANTOM.   O hurry, Brand, Come with me!
BRAND.   Alas, I dream!

Brand is able to see that this image of Agnes is an illusion, and he is able to renounce temptation. He then declares himself free to embody his concept of willed action, to "live the vision into deed." He sees this act as the choice of life, and he sees his act as figural in the sense that his renunciation of appearance and election of pure will shall illuminate the lives of others. It is important to realize that Brand sees his act as light-giving: the realization of his ideal is a source of light, running counter to that pattern which exists in the play associating darkness with confusion, obscurity, and sensuality. However, that which tempts Brand—either for the sensual or the aesthetic—is seen in terms of light. Here,

however, he sees himself, or his act, as the source of
light. Agnes's temptation is seen by Brand as precisely
that, a temptation. After her final words—"Die! Earth
can no longer use you!"—he identifies her as the falcon:

> *Away it flew, hunting through the dense mist,*
> *Flew on its great keen wings*
> *Out over the vast like a hawk.*

Certainly it is significant that Ibsen puts Agnes out into
the mist—the obscurity with which Brand has been
struggling. Gerd thinks, of course, that Brand is referring
to her falcon; and, strangely, Brand here confirms that
identification: "This time I have seen him." This unrealistic identification works to clarify that Gerd's escape
into the the sanctuary of the Ice Church is related to
Brand's ascent; both figures are pursued. Brand himself
directs her to arm against the falcon. He tells Gerd: "I
too was hunted." Brand also has been the victim of a
bird of prey, and the flight from this falcon is the struggle to which he refers. Brand clearly recognizes in this
scene that human experience itself is a consistent struggle, and his refusal to accept Gerd's identification of
him with the Christ seems to project his realization of
the inability of himself, as man, to triumph in that conflict. When Gerd asks him if he knows where he is, he
replies that he is below the first step of the ascent. Brand
suffers a real despair, sensing himself far from the realization of his vision; and even though he has denied the
possibility that his vision is a fantasy, the actual embodiment of it has not been his. He sees himself injured,
weak, vulnerable, far from "the ascent." At this point
of despair the mist dispells, and Brand realizes that he is
immediately below the black mountain peak, *Svartetind*,
in the Ice Church itself. Yet here within that image of
will realized, he objectifies his dream further forward,
longing for some distant place

> *. . . a thousand miles away from here!*
> *O, where I fervently yearn to be*
> *With light and sun and gentleness,*

> *With peace and stillness as in a church*
> *In life's summer kingdom.*

He wishes to fly to this idyllic place, recalling the phantom Agnes's temptation. From his despair he moves first into a dream of sensuality, calling up once again those images of calm, warmth, light; and then a reformation of the vision of the realization of the will in some kind of human action. There is the sense here that Brand's rededication is a rejection of his earlier renunciation. It is interesting that Ibsen describes Brand as "clean, radiant, clear, and as if reborn."

> *Through law, an ice-path opened—*
> *Then the summer sun from overhead!*
> *Until today I worked to become*
> *A blank tablet on which God could write.*
> *From today my life's illusion*
> *Shall yield, warm and opulent.*
> *The ice-crust breaks. I can weep,*
> *I can kneel—I can pray.*

Brand's "life's illusion" (*livsensdikt*) is resonant. *Dikt* is both "poem" and "lie" or "illusion." In *The Wild Duck*, Ibsen uses *livsløgnen* ("life-lie"), and in another place he pairs both terms: *Løgen og forbannet dikt* which translates "Lies and damned romancing." Brand seems to create a new myth within his consciousness which abandons the earlier myth of sacrifice and renunciation and associates itself not with the restrictive denial of seeing his identity only within divine action but in the dream of submission, warmth, and sensuality. For a moment, within the Ice Church, Brand seems to be released from his restrictive ethic. Part of this release is projected in the metaphors of yielding, dissolving, and melting. Gerd sees the clouds lifting away from the heights of the Ice Church and feels her own frozen memory melting—all in the warmth of Brand's tears. This warmth melts the ice which covers Brand's garments; and Gerd sees that dissolving case of ice in the image of a surplice being dropped from him: "Hot, thus his priest's robes slide/Down the sides of the glacier-priest."

These images of dissolution signal Brand's movement away from the myth to which he has dedicated his being. His own assurance that the ice crust is broken works with the insistent images of warmth coming from his hot tears to suggest strongly the disintegration of his fixed concentration upon his concept of the will. At this stage he seems to be attempting to create a new sense of form within a deliberate illusion—the "life's illusion" that carries with it all the qualities of freedom and warmth and light which he desires. However, this creation is only partial since it is at this moment that Gerd shoots the falcon and releases the power of the avalanche. Brand returns, at this point, to his sense of inherited guilt; answering Gerd's identification of the falcon: "Yes, each family's son is condemned/To death to expiate the family's sin!" Gerd conceives of the avalanche which is descending upon them as the descent of the falcon, then as the falcon transformed into a dove, and finally into the tent of heaven itself. Within this transformation, the image of sensuality which has been associated with the demonic abyss throughout the poem itself is metamorphosed into an image close to the "infinite arch of heaven"; and the fixed image of light becomes the source of darkness. Brand struggles against his coming death, seeing the newly achieved light destroyed:

> *Answer me, God, in death's abyss—*
> *Is there not a degree of redemption*
> *In the sufficient realization of a man's will?*

Brand is answered by the strange voice from the avalanche which says, "He is the God of love," as the snow crashes down upon them. The Ice Church remains a threat to the village throughout the play, and hovers overhead, keeping the valley in darkness. The sense of the place as sanctuary is illusory and the use of it as an escape releases its amazingly destructive force. Brand moves into the place of the Ice Church to be free from those irrational energies which would compromise his will; there he falls victim to a wild surge of energy represented by the avalanche itself—a destructive energy which kills him, Gerd, and (by implication) the whole village below. The image of the abyss is a metaphor of unrestrained and seemingly free sensuality—seen as rotten, festering, and cancerous. Early in *Brand* the Ice Church is seen as a "cavernous abyss," the only time this crucial metaphor of form is related to the abyss until Brand's final cry. But the Ice Church is merely the illusion of sanctuary; in reality it is the consistent threat of restrictive sensuality, needing only the slightest vibration to release its fettered energy. The movement to destroy the obvious and most clear image of sexuality, the falcon, releases the destructive energies of the unconscious itself. Here is the relationship between the height and the depth—the extremes which meet in Ibsen's drama of the the self. The sea offered Einar and Agnes the illusion of the possibility of escape to the sensuality and freedom of the south, and the heights offer Brand the illusion of an asceticism free from the threatening demands of sexuality; but neither offer of freedom is authentic. That freedom is not an aspect of Ibsen's reality; it can only exist as a created myth in the imagination of his hero, and the life of that myth is momentary since it is vulnerable to phenomenal reality. In *Brand*, the myth of order held in the image of the Ice Church posed over the abyss—precarious and threatening from the beginning of the play—has that momentary life. But the attempt to destroy the bird of prey, the concentrated symbol of sexuality, destroys the illusory form; and, in the avalanche, form becomes the abyss.

2

Peer Gynt

Brand is the imitation of a consciousness which is the focal point of strong pressures, and the tension of that play, despite its length, is almost unrelieved. Brand struggles with opposing desires throughout the work, and the attention of the play rarely leaves that conflict. *Peer Gynt* is close in time to *Brand*, and it is considered by many to be a companion work. However, *Peer Gynt* is a very different kind of play. In the first place, *Peer Gynt* uses an open, episodic plot which ranges far in time and place. While the concentration remains fixed upon its protagonist, the tension is diffused in the elaborations of scenic detail and the amazing variety of the hero's experiences. In the middle section of the play these experiences merely accumulate; they do not intensify Peer's struggle for identity. *Peer Gynt*'s relationship to reality is even more significant to the contrast with *Brand*. Nothing in Brand works to emphasize its conventionality other than the poetic language which attempts to intensify the events which are dramatized; that is, *Brand* makes the assumption that it is dealing with human experience realistically. On the other hand, *Peer Gynt* itself is a fantasy; and at various points in the action Ibsen calls attention to its unreality, identifying the play as artifice rather than reality.

An excellent illustration of the difference between the way in which *Brand* insists upon confronting the painfulness of reality and the way in which *Peer Gynt* distances us from that suffering occurs early in the second play. The play begins with Peer's exciting narration of a marvelous experience from which he has apparently just returned. This wildly romantic lie is an extremely interesting and beautiful version of Ibsen's predominant spatial metaphor—the vision of the contrasting halves of the world, the heights seen as an infinite arch and the depths as a seething abyss. In *Brand* this metaphoric landscape is the manifestation of a crucial division in consciousness; in *Peer Gynt* it is used playfully. The psychic experience this scenic metaphor embodies is frightening, but our emotional response to it is controlled by the dramatic fact of its fantasy.

> *Along the ridge he and I*
> *Cut through the air.*
> *I never rode such a colt.*
> *As we hurtled forward,*
> *The heights glistened like the sun.*
> *Brown eagles' backs swam*
> *In the wide, dizzying abyss*
> *Midway between us and the lakes;*
> *They fell behind like specks of dust.*
> *Ice flows cracked and broke against the cliffs*
> *But there was no rumble to hear;*
> *Merely whirling spirits who sprang up*
> *And danced; they sang, they went*
> *In circles in a fantasy of sight and sound.*
> *. . . Suddenly,*
> *Upon a dizzying sudden steep,*
> *A male ptarmigan, flapping,*
> *Cackling, frightened, appeared*
> *From a crag where he had hid*
> *Close upon the ridge before the stag's feet.*
> *The reindeer swung around, and*
> *Suddenly gave a heavenward leap*
> *Out over the abyss with us both.*
> *Behind us was the mountain's black walls,*
> *Underneath us the bottomless abyss.*

First we passed through layers of clouds
Then pierced a flock of gulls which went
Flying, screaming through the air in all directions.
Downward, without pause, we fell together.
But in the depths something glistened
Whitish as a reindeer's belly.
Mother, it was our own image
Which through the mountain lake calm
Rushed up against the water's surface
In that same wild speed
With which we downward sped.

Here, as in *Brand,* the ascent is terrifying and yet strangely fascinating; but here the act is not the manifestation of the will of the hero or even the fantasy of a willed act. This imaginative story is a profound exploration, in a condensed form, of the quality of Peer's sense of freedom. He sees himself as the rider of a powerful and magnificent steed; he is carried along, the patient of another energy, the coursing power of the marvelous animal. The ride ends in a fall through clouds into the depths of the lake. This clear image focuses a regressive movement, made more clear by the startling realization that the depths are, in reality, the reflection of one's own image which appears to be rushing up to meet the self.

In *Brand* the hero's confrontation with the actual content of the metaphor of the abyss is consistently avoided until it cannot be escaped in the final scene. The avalanche, as an image of suddenly released energy, is certainly a displacement of the abyss, but that resolution is not elaborated beyond the recognition that Brand must ultimately confront these energies as they destructively demand release at the moment of his death. *Brand* is able to disclose Ibsen's truth that the frightening energies embodied in the metaphor of the abyss exist within the individual consciousness and are not external forces. But that disclosure is indirect, worked out through complexities of language and dramatic structure. *Peer Gynt* has its own complex and painful disclosures, but the form of the play, its deliberate and conscious use of un-reality, softens the blow of those revelations. The un-threatening playfulness of *Peer Gynt* offers an implicit protection from its truths in the sense that the form itself suggests to the reader that the imaginative experience is fanciful and not a direct confrontation with the nature of human experience. Peer's fantasy itself, seen within the play as a lie, provides another layer of protection and another means of insulating us from the pain of the recognition that the confrontation with the abyss is, in reality, a confrontation with the self.

Peer Gynt is one of those works which moves from one mode to another and carries its meaning primarily in that transition. The work begins within the form of romance, building upon the romantic conception of a hero, despised and estranged from society, who emerges into an exceptional personality, accomplishing a variety of quests and becoming the emperor of his dreams in at least a limited sense. However, there is an uneasy and equivocal tension in this play between the romantic and the ironic view of its hero, and the play shifts in tone in the second half, assuming a satiric attitude toward its hero. Yet once again in the final scenes of the play, Peer's suffering becomes the focus of our identification as he suffers painful recognitions about the nature of himself and his relationship to a hostile world. *Peer Gynt* dram-atizes a search for self-sufficiency, a realization of the will as power. However, that quest is a search for the self which reveals that the self is a void. Peer learns that his acceptance of freedom has been just the opposite of his intention, that it has been dependence upon the random processes and the unceasing change of circumstance which eventually destroys the concept of an integral and continuous selfhood. However, that recognition does not close the play; instead the play resolves with Solveig's reunion with her beloved in a complex, equivocal, and ambiguous romantic vision.

In *Brand* the hero also suffers a painful reality, and we

have discussed his action as the embodiment of a mythical concept of reality which he has created in reaction to
that pain. In *Peer Gynt* the movement to transform the
nature of reality in an imaginative act is even clearer.
Ibsen establishes that Peer and his mother, Ase, use
fantasy to escape the deprivation and isolation of their
experience:

> . . . *Little Peer and I sat at home together.*
> *We knew of no better remedy than forgetting;*
> . . . .
> *And try our best to push such thoughts away from us.*
> *One person uses liquor, another tries illusion;*
> *Oh yes! So we used fairy tales*
> *Of princes and trolls and all kinds of creatures.*

The early scenes of the play show that this transformation of reality into a fantasy is Peer's imaginative pattern. The reality of his situation is clear: he is the only
child of a widow whose once wealthy husband wasted
their money in benevolent but foolish good living. His
own foolish pranks have estranged the community. Peer
deals with this alienation by creating a fantasy life which,
of course, he boasts about, further irritating his neigh-
bors. The primary difference between Brand and Peer
Gynt is that Peer's imaginative act is the careless ro-
manticizing of experience rather than the embodiment
of some concept of reality. Illusion in this work is im-
plemented differently. Brand's action is the manifestation of his sense of will; Peer's action is the revaluation
of past experience into some illusion which transforms
pain into pleasure.

Peer Gynt concentrates initially upon the phenom-
enology of experience. The objects of his desire change
from being the focus of his energy to the focus of his
disgust, revealing the transformation implicit in sexual
processes. For example, Peer's response to his sexual use
of Ingrid is a strong guilt which voices itself in his cruel
rejection of her. She is the bride who wished at one time
to marry him, offering him the incentive of her family's

wealth. When Ase tells Peer that Ingrid is marrying someone else, Peer decides to go to the wedding. But he pretends that the situation is different, transporting his rejection and poverty within his imagination into grandeur and obeisance:

> Peer Gynt rides first, followed by many men.
> His steed is crested in silver and shod in gold.
>
> . . . .
>
> Everyone can recognize
> Emperor Gynt and his thousand squires.

At the wedding, Peer attempts to help the cowardly bridegroom by breaking into Ingrid's room, but he kidnaps the bride instead and, with probable encouragement, rapes her. But once he has used her she no longer holds value for him and he discards her:

PEER GYNT. Go! Go back where you came from!
    Quickly! Back to your father!
INGRID. Dear one—!
PEER GYNT. Be quiet!
INGRID. You can't possibly mean
    What you say.
PEER GYNT. I can and I do.
INGRID. First seduced—and then denied!
PEER GYNT. And what terms have you to offer?
INGRID. Haegstad farm and even more.
PEER GYNT. Do you have a prayer book in your
    kerchief?
    Do you have golden tresses down to your shoulders?
    Do you lower your eyes quickly down to your
    apron?
    Do you hold onto your mother's skirt?
    Answer!

Peer describes Solveig in this critical passage; she is a young girl whom he met at the wedding and in his imagination she becomes the image of innocence, the most perfect object of desire. The following scenes repeat this pattern of action and response: Peer exper-

iences a series of sexual adventures, followed by a strong
sense of guilt and a return to the image of Solveig's innocence. The images of aggressive sexuality are progressively intense: first there is the willing Ingrid, agreeing to
her rape; then there are the three cowherd girls, looking
for exotic trolls to substitute for their absent men. The
blatant sexuality of this scene is obvious and the demanding women provide a clear contrast to Solveig's innocence
and patience. The next scene presents the guilty Peer,
desirous of cleansing:

> There soar two brown eagles.
> The wild geese are flying to the south.
> And I must trudge and stumble here
> Up to my knees in the mud and filth. (springing up)
> I will go with them! I will wash myself clean
> In the bath of the sharpest wind!
> Up high I will immerse myself gently
> In that shining christening font;
> I will fly over the farmhouses;
> I will fly until I have cleansed myself.

Within the recurrent spatial metaphor, the heights are
seen as part of an antithesis between the ascetic and the
erotic; again, however, the heights are not merely an objective in themselves, but an escape from sexual experience and guilt.

The Woman in Green is one of Ibsen's most clearly
erotic images; and her double identity clarifies Peer's
imaginative act of transposing the nature of reality. This
sense of double identity, the transformation from the
attractive to the repelling, is part of Peer's response to
Ingrid and the three girls. Here that ambivalence becomes tangible in the dual character of the Troll Princess and her kingdom.

> Everything which is ours has a double form:
> When you come to my father's palace,
> It might easily happen that you consider
> It to be an ugly pile of stones.

The strangely supernatural episode in the Hall of the Troll King is an imaginative projection of the central act of this interesting play. This scene explores the filth and bestiality of the Troll Kingdom and the implicit hostility of the trolls toward Peer as a human being. The temptation to marry the Troll Princess is not only erotic but is based upon Peer's desire for wealth and power; her dowry includes half of the Troll Kingdom before the death of the king and its entirety when he dies. But the demands put upon Peer are telling:

First you must promise that you will never pay heed
To anything which lies outside the boundaries of these
*   cliffs;*
You must avoid the day, deeds, and every spot of sun-
*   light.*

Peer must also give up the human objective, "Man, to yourself be true," and supplant it with the troll's motto, "Troll, to yourself be—enough." Each stimulus which he perceives is disgusting, and yet he attempts to transform it within his imagination into something of value: disgusting drink, repellent food, the actual presence of the Troll Princess as she dances in the form of a cow. In order to make this process an easier task, the Troll King declares that he is going to "scratch [him] in the left eye slightly" to make his vision "oblique" and cut out his right eye so that all he looks upon "will seem to be elegant and distinguished." Peer objects to this final demand and escapes the trolls, having been beaten severely by them—avoiding death only because they are frightened away by the bells in the valley.

This scene seems to be a playful fantasy of the abyss—that metaphor which in Ibsen's other plays carries fear as well as a paradoxical attraction. Peer's escape from the Troll Kingdom—its darkness and bestiality—seems complete, but the Dovre King reminds him of the threatening presence of the child who will be born from his desire for the Troll Princess: "one thing is certain—what's done is done, and furthermore your offspring will grow up; such mongrels mature amazingly fast." The relationship between Ibsen's concept of sexuality and the image of the trolls is clear in *Peer Gynt*; the sexual nature of the trolls is clarified in the cowherd girls' search for trolls to substitute for their human lovers; and the temptation of The Woman in Green is also clearly sexual. The sense of threat—the threat to the will in circumscribing power and the threat to perception in the injured ability to apprehend reality—is shown here as the danger of the abyss. This adventure which seems to be an assertion of Peer's individuality is, metaphorically, a clarification of sexuality as a demonic force within his own nature. When he recognizes what marriage to the Troll Princess would mean, he rejects that act as a surrender which would threaten his freedom.

> *To know that one can never free oneself*
> *And not even die as a decent human being can do,*
> *To go as mountain troll all one's days*
> *And never to go back again . . .*
> *But that is something which I could never agree to.*

Of course, Peer fails to recognize that the actual presence of the trolls merely signals those forces within himself to which he continually submits. The tangible, concretely manifested threat of this scene, however, is balanced by Peer's confrontation with the strange and elusive identity of the Great Boyg in the next scene.

Peer's experience with the Great Boyg is an encounter with an obstacle which cannot be seen nor passed through. This creature is a peculiar image, "slimy, fibrous, no form." It does not attack; it provides an impassable atmosphere. Peer's attempt to pass through the Boyg is unsuccessful until he evokes the image of Solveig—referring to her lowered head, her blushes, and her prayer book. This memory is reinforced by the sound of church bells and the singing of psalms, and the following scene reveals that Solveig has indeed saved Peer.

It is obvious by this point in the drama that Peer's

experience is not based upon a simple conflict between illusion and reality, but upon a complex of forces difficult to put into concrete images. He desires a kind of romantic heroism which will transcend the reduction and rejection of his real experience, and yet that desire for transcendence does not manifest itself in the creation of a myth similar to Brand's. Rather, Peer's experience avoids the transcendent which would isolate him from human processes and he "loses himself" in experience itself, in participating in these processes. Peer is the embodiment of phenomenal experience, and that experience cannot be given the formal order of the mythical since it is not the fulfillment of an order which has either been created or comprehended in the consciousness. The details perceived in direct experience, unless ordered in some mythical conception, cannot be comprehended. Ibsen's response to the phenomenal is ambiguous. Sensual experience is, of course, a recurring temptation, but he also distances it in the plays with the condemnation of such adjectives as *filthy*, *slimy*, and the critical *formless*. The primary way in which Ibsen works to project a negative attitude toward sexuality in *Peer Gynt* is to insist that the value of the object for which Peer lusts is illusory. The pattern repeats itself with some insistence, clarified most directly in the grotesque presence of The Woman in Green. The Woman in Green is a flexible character whose identiy can undergo a metamorphosis to clarify Peer's own attitude toward her; or, perhaps more clearly, her changing identity clarifies the dynamics of the sexual process itself, seen negatively. Solveig is the opposite image, unchanging and infinitely innocent. She renounces her family and comes to Peer in the forest where he is hiding as a fugitive after his crime of raping Ingrid. Here it seems possible for Peer to realize an actual happiness. Peer sees Solveig offering him her innocence and a sanctuary from evil. His response to her attempts to move away from the erotic:

Now I will need no bolts against evil thoughts.
If you dare to enter here and live with this hunter,

I know that this hut will become consecrated,
Solveig! Let me look at you! Not too near!
I'll only look at you! O, where you are is light and purity.

. . . .

I shall never soil you. I'll hold you
At arms' length away from me, you are so clean and
    warm.

Immediately after Solveig comes to Peer, he meets The Woman in Green, transformed into a grotesque old crone. She is accompanied by a distorted and ugly child, the demonic product of Peer's desire; and she tells Peer that she demands to be with him and Solveig. Her presence, which is the embodiment of his guilt, makes the relationship with Solveig impossible:

> *It is no good; were my arms as long*
> *As pine branches or spruce limbs—*
> *I know I could not hold her far enough away*
> *To set her down from me unsoiled and pure.*

Peer's movement away from Solveig is analogous to Brand's renunciation of Agnes and later actions in Ibsen's plays which work toward sustaining a personal image of innocence, keeping that figure unsullied and protected from experience. Peer's course continues to be unformed, unshaped, using and exploiting opportunities which present themselves immediately, concentrating upon immediate satisfactions. That which remains for him constant, unchanged, is the image of Solveig. She is the manifestation of the mythical, and he renounces her. However, that renunciation is ambiguous because it is only the renunciation of Solveig as part of his experience which makes it possible for her to remain unchanged, suspended in innocence. Sexual use is the consumption of experience. In the spending of desire in the sexual event, the event consumes itself; and the sexual object itself seems to change identity as emotion resolves from acute desire to satisfaction. The very consumption which the appetite demands destroys the appetite and so disintegrates the source of value. Desire regenerates, but in *Peer Gynt* Ibsen puts the emphasis upon the movement from desire to repulsion. The sexual objects which Peer confronts are used and then discarded as repulsive to him. By renouncing Solveig, Peer protects her from this process. Solveig functions for Peer as a constant. She is an ideal removed from time and process in an experience which is otherwise unstructured and immediate. Peer is unable to make her part of his phenomenal experience, and she remains innocent.

Immediately after the scene in which Peer renounces Solveig, leaving her to wait for him in the forest, he returns to his dying mother and once more they play the game of fantasy. Peer leads her to her death within the illusion of driving her to a splendid feast at Soria-Maria Castle. It is significant that his renunciation of Solveig is balanced by the death of his mother; and this death marks the end of the first movement of the play with the departure of Peer Gynt for "the sea . . . and farther away."

Peer Gynt's attitude toward its hero seems to change in act 4. The romantic carefree spirit and the indifference toward consequence which were somewhat appealing in Peer's youth are, in middle age, seen to be exploitative, selfish, and immature. Peer's tendency to transform the immediate circumstance into a fantasy of his exceptional nature is seen as the rationalization of a man unable to deal with his experience. We see Peer in the first scene of act 4 after a successful career as a trader. He has shipped Negro slaves to America and idols to China, and to ease his conscience, he also shipped missionaries to China. He eventually gave up trade and established a plantation in a southern state. Peer's recital of his experience makes it sound fragmented; that is, his experience is not unified by a single vision which provides him with a consistent sense of identity. On the contrary, he explains his "success" in terms of freedom rather than commitment:

> *Success demands the art of daring,*
> *The art of possessing the courage of the deed,*

Which is: To stand free
Of life's deceitful snares,
To know assuredly that each day
Is not the end of daily strife—
To make certain that there is always
A bridge left open which can lead you back.
This theory sustained me;
It has qualified my whole course of action;
It is a theory which I inherited from
My family in my childhood home.

This is not a vision of life which carries him forward, but is, rather, a device to offer him a way out of the danger of one situation and into a safer one. It is the antithesis of Brand's idealism which invests all of the energies into the single act. Peer's attempt to convince Mr. Cotton, Monsieur Ballon, Herr van Eberkopf, and Herr Trump-teterstraale to help the Turks in the Greek and Turkish conflict is a practical maneuver rather than an idealistic act and inspires the wrath of these men who themselves are selfish and exploitative but see themselves as fulfilling some kind of mythical identity which, in their imaginations, would justify their actions. These men themselves trick Peer and steal his yacht, and we see Peer in despair as he finds his ship, fortune, and opportunity leaving; but then he sees the ship explode and realizes that this theft has been his protection. This dramatic device gives Ibsen a chance to show Peer's reaction to his specific environment and to develop Peer's own concept of experience after he has been stripped of all resources other than his own body and imagination.

Ibsen does not show Peer as a successful trader or plantation owner. Instead, he presents the deterioration of Peer's success; and the course of Peer's experience becomes progressively ludicrous—Peer hounded by apes, Peer dressing in a sultan's costume and enacting the role of a prophet, Peer being tricked by a slave girl.

The episode with Anitra is clearly analogous to his relationship with The Woman in Green; he imagines both sensual experiences as being other than what they are in reality. The primary difference between them, of course, is that Anitra does not desire Peer but rather exploits him for his wealth. Both erotic relationships use the image of empire. Recall that the Troll Princess offered the Troll Empire as part of her temptation. The second episode more clearly projects the eroticism of that image:

> It [To live] is to float
> Dryshod down the river of time,
> Becoming heroic and wealthy by your own acts.
> Only through manly strength can I be
> What I am, my dear little one!
> Aged eagles lose their feathers, . . .
> Aged crones lose their teeth,
> Aged fogeys get withered hands—
> Each receives a withered soul.
> Youth! Youth! I will reign,
> As a sultan, passionately over all—
> Not upon Gyntiana's banks,
> Under palmleafs and vines—
> But on the foundation of freshness
> Which rests in a woman's virgin thoughts.
> You see now, my little girl,
> Why I have graciously ensnared you,
> Why I have chosen your heart,
> Established, if I must say so myself,
> There my being's caliphate.
> I will possess your longings.
> Omnipotent in my kingdom of love!

Peer's relationship with Anitra is clearly an attack on the nature of time itself, and his ridiculous behavior in this scene reveals his desire for youth and the folly of his attempt to transcend time within the creation of an imaginary world. Peer's desire has been to experience reality; but subject to the processes of aging, he seeks to stop time—to pass "dryshod down the river of time." This section of *Peer Gynt* exposes two difficult but rewarding concerns with which Ibsen deals: first, the acute need for comprehension or, at least, illusions of comprehending the nature of reality; and second, the related, and perhaps parallel, desire to acquire, encompass, or imprison the object of desire. Peer's relationship with Anitra exposes his sexual greed and his fear of the processes of time. Fearing her loss, he creates a rhetorical fantasy of imprisoning her within his adoration:

> *Omnipotent in my kingdom.*
> *You must be mine alone.*
> *I will imprison you,*
> *Binding you with gold and precious stones. . . .*
> *Your hair dark as midnight,*
> *And your beauty, beyond destruction,*
> *Like Babylonian gardens, shall*
> *Lead me to a sultan's kingdom.*

Anitra proves to be a transient and unimprisonable sexual object, and Peer's desire then manifests itself in his illusion of finding the mysterious sphinx, of being, in fact, *Fortolkerne's Keiser*, "the Emperor of Interpretation," who shall explain reality. Part of the difficulty of the Egyptian episodes in *Peer Gynt* is their structural complexity; the scenes work on a series of levels, and perhaps suffer from an unclear or unfocused perspective. By this point in the play, of course, Peer is the focus of the play's satire rather than the focus of identification as he was at the beginning of the play. His characterization remains ambiguous, however, since we still respond to the essentially human quality of his desires despite the fact that his greed and folly are seen ironically. His fragmented and improvised illusions of his own significance and ability are seen as perversions of the imagination.

The image of the mysterious sphinx is clearly ironic, recalling as it does Sophocles' *Oedipus Tyrannus*. The clear discrepancy between Oedipus's unrelenting search for the truth of his identity and Peer's psychic refusal to confront the nature of his, is comic.

The scene within the lunatic asylum in Cairo is, in many ways, a black-comic episode. Peer's irrationality, which masks itself as realism and reason, is seen for what it is, a self-concerned withdrawal from reality. Peer sees the madmen as having abandoned or lost their sense of the self; and, the keeper—Begriffebfeldt—sees them as precisely the opposite:

> It is here that men are themselves completely,
> Themselves and nothing else;
> Proceeding, as themselves, under full sail.
> Each closes himself up in the cask of the self,
>
> . . . .
>
> None has a tear for the other's suffering,
> None has appreciation for the other's ideas; we are
> Ourselves, in thought and word,
> Ourselves, to the very furthest limit.
> And consequently, should we name our Emperor,
> It is clear you are the right man.

Each of the madmen Peer encounters in the asylum is fixed upon some illusory identity, an illusory identity which is a denial of the limitations of his real nature or position. The final figure he meets is a grotesque comic person, a minister of state who sees himself as an unsharpened pen. Peer's responses in kind to this figure's tragic declarations are themselves telling: "I am a sheet of paper which has never been written on." Peer also returns to the image of the reindeer jumping from the heights and never hitting the solid ground, taking us back to the fantasy with which the play opened—that narrative which embraced the typical metaphor of space and revealed that the fall into the abyss is a confrontation with the self. The macabre quality of this scene is intensified as the deluded minister of state cuts his throat, under the illusion that he has sharpened himself as a pen, and Peer Gynt is crowned Emperor of the Self as he swoons in the mud.

Ibsen's perspective toward this material seems closer to irony and satire than in those works which assume a quality of realism; and that freedom from the demands of plausibility allows him to work more playfully with

some of the concepts which inform the other plays more
threateningly. The deluded suicide of Hussein, who kills
himself convinced that he is fulfilling his actual identity,
bears some relation to Brand who, fixed upon his mythical view of himself, subjects himself to a danger which
does kill him. This comic exposition of the self-destructive nature of illusion voices part of the ambiguous attitude which is present in the more serious plays, qualifying and compounding their resolution.

In both *Brand* and *Emperor and Galilean* the balance
between the mythical and the phenomenal perspectives
is delicately, if precariously, maintained. The resolving
moments of both plays clarify that while the mythical
concepts held in the consciousness of its heroes have
proved to be inadequate and ultimately destructive, the
human consciousness needs a mythology or a cosmology
in order to conceive of itself, to participate in experience
creatively, and to develop a concept of time. In both
Brand and *Emperor and Galilean* that personal myth is
an increasingly fixed and static notion of the self and
works toward the sense of the self enclosing the whole
world in a fantasy of self-identification. The fixed quality
of that personal myth is part of its destructiveness and
yet is the quality of its strength. In *Peer Gynt*, there is
no sense of a consistent and integral personal mythology.
Each experience is the immediate ground for an individual interpretation. Peer attempts to transcend each event
imaginatively, but these interpretations provide a fragmented, incoherent, disorganized sequence of illusions
rather than a real mythology which is the basis of action.

The last part of *Peer Gynt* is built upon a sequence of
realizations experienced by its hero. Peer consistently
responds to reality by creating an illusion which accom-
modates the situation. For example, Peer comes upon
the funeral of the man who had cut off his finger to
evade military service. The sermon given by the priest is
a complex and detailed explanation of that act and its
consequences. That life, however, directly contrasts with
Peer's: it is contained, restricted, dedicated; filled with

suffering, self-consciousness, and guilt. And yet, in the words of the priest, *this man had been himself*. Peer sees this statement as a biblical justification for his own life, and we see that he is creating an illusion that his life has been the embodiment of his will and that he has achieved a clear selfhood.

In the next scene, Peer discovers an auction attended by an aged Aslak and others. Several of Peer's things are sold, and there is much joking about the old Peer who has become something of a legendary figure of ridicule. When Peer asks them what they know of Peer Gynt, an old man reports that he was hanged. Then Peer tells a story about the devil in San Francisco who hid a real pig under his coat and then pretended to make pig noises in imitation, and was subject to the criticism of the exaggeration of his performance. Peer seems to be saying here that it is difficult to project to the imaginations of others a clear sense of what reality is and that to tell them of the reality of Peer would be to bring forth the charge of exaggeration. In the next scene, Peer grubs for wild onions and constructs a clear-cut metaphor in the relationship between the layers of an onion and the fragmentation of his own identity; however, when he comes to the center, he finds no core: "To the innermost core it is/Nothing but layers—only smaller and smaller." This image moves toward the concept that there is no integral self which can be identified and made constant; but rather that identity is fragmented, realized in the specific situation, but having no continuing integrity. This is more a phenomenal sense of identity than a mythical in which being is the enactment of a sense of order, a structured sequence of events which forms part of the larger pattern in a comprehensible vision of reality. This is the most despairing of the concepts of the nature of human experience in the play; and it is developed in some of the remaining scenes, although the romantic form of the play does not allow *Peer Gynt* to end with that despairing perspective.

The sense of selfhood as fragmented, realized only in

specific deeds, unrelated, sequential, and diffuse, is am-
plified in the next scene which is clearly a manifestation
of Peer's own vision of his personal history as a wasteland: "*Night. Moor. A forest fire has ravaged. Charred
tree trunks and ashes extend over the scene. White mist
hangs here and there in the forest.*" This burned forest
is the image of the reality of the present in clear antithesis to the forest in which Peer built his hut, the forest
which was a sanctuary from punishment for him and
which could have provided a shelter for his life with
Solveig. That difference is defined in his speech:

> *Ashes, mist, dust in the wind,*
> *This is enough to build with!*
> *Stench and rottenness within;*
> *All heaped in a whited sepulchre.*

Each of the apparitions which comes to him in this
location—the balls of thread, the withered leaves, the
unsung songs—are images of his wasted life which, un-
integrated, is subject to rot, decomposition, and waste.

Peer's next disillusionment comes in his encounter
with the demonic button molder who tells him that his
being will be melted down—that his self is neither vital
nor exceptional enough to be punished specifically in
hell, but that in death he will

> . . . *have to be dissolved*
> *like a speck of dust in an insignificant body of matter*
> . . . *annihilating all that makes a Gynt.*

Peer attempts to gain recognition of his identity as a
sinner in order to maintain his sense of the integrity of
the self, to keep from being lost in the button molder's
amalgamation of souls. His encounter with the aged and
failing Dovre King provides his most painful recognition.
The old man tells him that his escape from the control
of the trolls was an illusion, and that in reality he did
submit to the king's demands:

PEER GYNT. Yes, you tempted me, seductively—
      But I ultimately stood firm against that tempta-
      tion.
      And that is precisely how a man is recognized
      It is the concluding verse which resolves the poem.
DOVRE KING. But the conclusion was just the op-
      site of what you think! . . .
      When you abandoned the mountains, you left
      With my motto inscribed behind your ear. . . .
      . . . The crucial difference
      Between men and trolls is contained in the strong
      words:
      Troll, to yourself be enough!
PEER GYNT (*giving a shriek*). *Enough!*
DOVRE KING. And throughout your whole life
      You have lived fulfilling it.

This scene makes explicit what is implicit in Ibsen's
frightening image of the abyss. The image of the Troll
Kingdom revealed the abyss as the source of both temptation and terror. One aspect of the terror of the abyss is
the loss of the sense of the self as determining—the surrender to instinctive energy seen as a loss of unique selfhood. The Troll Kingdom, and specifically The Woman
in Green, is a culmination of a series of images of Peer's
sexuality and his response to sexuality. The Dovre King
reveals to Peer that he has not escaped from the irrational
aspect of his own being—those energies which would
work against a sense of his experience being the manifestation of his conscious will. Peer's perception was damaged by the Dovre King, making him see the objects of
his desire as beautiful despite their reality. The disintegration of Peer's image of the Gyntian self is an acute
recognition, and Peer confronts the truth that the de-
monism of the Dovre King is an irrationality within his
own being.

   (A shooting star flashes by: he nods after it.)
   Regards from Peer Gynt, brother falling star!
   To shine, be extinguished, and lost in the abyss.

(Composes himself fearfully and goes deeper into the forest, stands still, and then he cries out.)
Is there no one, no one in the whole multitude—
No one in the abyss, no one in heaven!
(He comes forward further down, throws his hat on the path and tears his hair. By degrees he grows calmer.)

So indescribably poor can a soul go
Back to nothingness in the gray mist.
Beautiful earth, don't be angry
That I trample your grass for no purpose.
Beautiful sun, you have wasted
Your rays of light upon a hut empty of people.
There was no one there to warm and bless;
The owner, they say, was never home.
Beautiful sun and beautiful earth,
It was foolish of you to nourish and warm my mother
Spirit is miserly and nature extravagant.
Paying for one's birth with life itself is expensive.

Immediately after Peer's recognition of his unconscious submission to those irrational energies which operate against self-determination, he explains his despair. First of all, he bears witness to the impermanence of his experience—the sudden bright course of a falling star which has a momentary life and then becomes as nothing, returning to the "gray mists." Frequently Ibsen's heroes fight through mists as manifestations of obscurity and doubt. This metaphor of obscurity is the direct antithesis of the concept of form, comprehensibility, or order.

Peer's description of his final act—to climb to the heights to see the sunrise and view the glories of the earth, "the promised land"—is extremely interesting. This, of course, is the metaphoric action chosen by so many of Ibsen's heroes—and, frequently, is an action taken by them in the creation of a final illusion after all the other illusions have been disintegrated or failed as crucial strategies. Here the image of ascent is clearly the product of an acute despair, a despair caused by Peer's recognition that the self which he identified as his own being does not exist. After this moment, Peer hears the church people singing on the road: "Blessed morning/ When the tongue of God's kingdom/Hits earth like flaming steel!" Peer then refuses to look out at the vision of the promised land which, for him, has become "wasteland and emptiness." And he conceives of himself as having been dead long before his actual death. This vision of human experience and the world which contains it is certainly demonic; and if *Peer Gynt* resolved here, the work would certainly be ironic. Peer's vision of a fruitful and beautiful promised land is replaced with a despairing vision of the world itself as a devastated inferno—and himself as disintegrated into that wasteland, becoming one with the waste.

A complex of concepts is at work here, and yet it is difficult to isolate each one, holding it up for view, since the strength of the scene is the balance among them. The pain of sensing the loss of identity voices itself in the metaphor of melting (related certainly to that strong metaphor in *Emperor and Galilean* of merging with the primal deep); the illusion of being able to see the world from the heights disintegrates. This metaphor of seeing the world is a particularly meaningful one for Ibsen. It relates to a concept of being able to understand the world and to attain the object of desire, seeing, comprehending, encompassing, possessing. This vision is, in Peer's imagination, "the promised land." The sense of possession, achievement, comprehension, the gaining of a personal cosmology is the objective and the illusion of Ibsen's heroes. The reality is the desert waste. Peer's realization of this reality voices itself in his sense of death in life or, rather, his fear of death in life. "I am afraid of being dead long before my death." This metaphor, of course, is voiced fully in the later plays, culminating in the image of the "dead" Irene in *When We Dead Awaken*.

Too little attention has been paid by critics to the complexity of the resolution of Ibsen's plays—resolutions which keep the difficult concepts that have been in the play throughout the work sharply focused, and yet which do not resolve them in any single perspective. The plays frequently end with uneasy and difficult equivocations. In discussing *Peer Gynt*, for example, it is possible to describe its dramatic structure as a romance. Peer's romantic quest for the self has lead him through a series of exceptional adventures along a circular route to the point at which his innocent lover and his mother meet; there, threatened by a demonic force which would convince him of the failure of his quest, he finds his identity and place in seeing himself as the child of God the Father. The play ends with a clear sense of return and the final image of Peer and Solveig establishing the same relationship as Peer and Ase, quietly dreaming and playing together as mother and son.

Solveig has maintained her vigil from youth to old age —she is the image of innocence suspended, and the suggestion is clear that Peer's real identity is maintained within that pure and unsullied imagination. However, that notion of the hero's discovery of his actual self is ambiguous. Consider the language and visual imagery of their reunion:

SOLVEIG.   It is he! It is he! Praised be God!
     (*She gropes for him.*)
PEER GYNT.   Tell me where I have sinned so evilly.
SOLVEIG.   You have sinned in nothing, my only boy.
     (*She gropes for him again and finds him.*)

Peer is identified by a *blind* Solveig, and that strong visual image of the unseeing Solveig groping toward Peer provides an implicit qualification. It is, perhaps, only her image of Peer who is the child of God the Father and who has received the pardon bestowed because of a mother's prayers. Ibsen gives the stage directions that "A ray of light passes over him."

Solveig's love, the love of an innocent woman, is also seen once more within the image of sanctuary, as Peer cries, threatened with death:

My mother, my wife; innocent woman!
O, hide me, hide me, within you!
(He clings to her and hides his face in her lap—
A long silence . . .)

Within the imagery of a romantic apocalypse or the *illusion* of romantic apocalypse

(The sun rises.) SOLVEIG (sinigng quietly).
Sleep my dearest boy!
I will rock you, I will watch over you.

The button molder, however, is still a threatening presence; yet he does not state clearly that he will claim Peer. The threat remains an equivocation: "We shall meet at the last crossroads, Peer; and so *then* we'll see—! I'll say no more." Solveig continues her song, lit by the sun: "I will rock you, I will watch over you. Sleep and dream, my dearest boy." The final focus, of course, is upon the reunited image of Peer and Solveig with its sense of personal integration, and yet that final concentration is also the image of the dreaming Peer, the hero hidden from the threat of reality, protected and nurtured and allowed to continue within the sanctuary of illusion. Possibly this work closes within the image of the romantic hero fulfilling an archetypal incestuous wish; and yet, viewing this resolution from a consideration of what we could call Ibsen's personal mythology, this transition in the image of Solveig from lover to mother is also a means of diminishing the threat of sexuality.

In terms which have frequently been discussed, *Peer Gynt* functions as a companion play to *Brand*, exploring the nature of instinctive experience as *Brand* explores the nature of willed experience. That antithesis is too patent a critical judgment: in both plays, sexuality is looked at from an ambivalent perspective—as the lure which tempts the hero into danger and as irrational and destructive. Irrationality is seen destroying the concept of the self, and the renunciation of sexuality is seen as necessary for the preservation of a vision of selfhood. Brand is led, through his fear, into the false sanctuary of the Ice Church; Peer is gathered into the sanctuary of his relationship with Solveig, which at best is an equivocal safety. The movement in both *Brand* and *Emperor and Galilean* to create myths of reality which contain a sense of a comprehensible universe is clear and, on one level, is the antithesis of Peer's active engagement in experience itself. And yet, Peer's illusion-making relates to the acts of Brand and Julian as well. He does hold a vision of himself as an exceptional human being, and in devious ways he does enact the content of the vision. Like them, he renounces the woman whose innocence he adores; and yet he does not renounce sexuality in general as Brand and Julian do. Peer Gynt finds that the sense of identity which he has achieved in his diffused experience is transient, and that, for him, identity is consistently reformed, transposed in his strategy of reconstructing the past reality into the present fantasy. However, there is no central core in this act of creating illusion; the quality of the illusion is based upon the content of the experience being rationalized. Brand creates a myth and then enacts that myth. Peer Gynt suffers experience, and then, from the substance of that experience, re-evaluates it, reforming it into some pleasurable kind of illusion. However, when Peer returns home, he discovers that the only cohesive identity he has is within the legend of Peer Gynt; he does have a mythical self, more consistent, surely, than that elaborated "Gyntian Self." However, this legendary or mythical self does not originate in the mind of Peer Gynt, and it is neither satisfying nor tangible; nor is it really comprehensible to him. However, what is satisfying and tangible is the reformation of his relationship to Solveig—the creature whom he has suspended in a mythical identity. Here, of course, he finds his identity as a child with a mother, or at least, the illusion of a return to his mother. This sense of a cyclical return and the attending resonances of rebirth and regeneration is part of the play's romantic structure, but that structure in itself is dense, holding ambiguities which qualify its form.

Peer Gynt is both a romance and a critique of romance at the same time. I do not think that the play is a self-parody in any strong sense, nor do I believe that Ibsen is playing fanciful games with his spectators or readers in a kind of literary or theatrical joke. *Peer Gynt* is not making fun of *Brand*, in that sense. Rather, the complexity and obvious freedom of the form or forms within the play are part of the exploration or at least the consideration of the ways in which consciousness deals with experience and, even more significantly, the multiplicity of levels on which that experience exists. There is a tangible sense of integration in the return of Peer to a kind of relationship with Solveig which existed before with Ase, and the fulfilling of a romantic archetypal pattern is a direct and immediate aspect of that final scene; and yet, at the same time, that interpretation of experience operates as an escape from the reality of the event. Peer is presented as a disillusioned old man, a failure who returns to his childhood scene embittered and afraid of death and who is comforted by an old woman whose life has been spent in futile patience, waiting for the return of her lover. The romantic sense of integration may be only one interpretation of that event, but it in itself is an aspect of reality because it exists as a strategy within consciousness itself. The ironic deprecation of that sense of integration also exists. Both interpretations live within the attitude of the play, and the movement among perspectives allows that complexity although it confuses the focus of our response to the work.

3

Emperor and Galilean

During his final moments, Peer Gynt grows closer to the typical Ibsenian hero and deals aggressively and self-consciously with those problems which torment the protagonists of Ibsen's more concentrated plays. Peer's consciousness is divided between a desire to see reality as comprehensible in a form in which the sight and the imagination can encompass it and an equally strong fear that there is no form of reality, that there is only waste and barrenness. Ibsen communicates this experience in a compressed passage which we should examine once more:

> I will ascend to the heights of the steepest mountain;
> I will see the sun rise one more time,
> Staring at the promised land until I am exhausted.
> Then the snow will bury me;
> And on this grave will be written the epitaph:
> "Here No One is buried."

Then, almost immediately, Peer cries that he will not look out at the promised land: "Never look there. It is wasteland and emptiness. I am afraid I have been dead long before my death."

Being able to see the world from the heights and encompass it within the imagination is a crucial metaphor in Ibsen's work; and the sense of staring at the world until the eyes are exhausted seems to be a repressed but powerful image of holding firm to a vision of a promised land and imposing that vision upon a reality. At this point, Peer refuses to attempt to maintain that vision, confronting instead the possibility that the promised land is itself a wilderness of waste and desert. The juxtaposition of two conceptions of that reality—the promised land and the barren desert—is a typical antithesis in Ibsen, and is related to the kind of psychic tension projected in *Emperor and Galilean*. Only within the experience of comprehension does the individual self seem to have a sense of identity. The fear of a loss of self-consciousness in *Peer Gynt* is obvious, especially in that sense of movement from affirming the reality of the promised land to being buried by the snow in a grave identified as that of *no one*. Then there is the fear of being melted down in the button molder's ladle, merging with a mass of unrealized identities. And yet the dread of anonymity and self-dissolution is not the only stimulus of fear. Peer is able to accept that at this point with, "And, after that—well, come what may," but the voices of the church singers remind him of the Christian vision of an afterlife, and his acute fear at the end of the scene derives from his apprehension that perhaps he will continue to suffer after death. His sense of the omnipresence of guilt destroys even the ambiguous comfort of the possibility of self-dissolution. Peer moves away, at this moment, from either an attempt to comprehend experience or to create an illusion of comprehension. *"He attempts to steal into the thickets, but finds himself standing at the crossroads."* His movement is the antithesis of the ascent to the mountaintops. He attempts to lose himself in the density of the thickets rather than move toward the clearer vision from the heights. Peer consistently evades the movement toward comprehension and his brief encounter with reality is a unique moment in the play.

Ibsen does not use Peer's imagination as the arena for the tension between phenomenal and mythical conceptions of reality; that tension informs the play only indirectly. However, in *Emperor and Galilean* Julian's consciousness sees itself in this divided way, although, as in

Brand, the process of confronting the nature of consciousness is a "blind groping." *Emperor and Galilean* is an uncomfortable, even frightening and hysterical work, because it focuses upon a consciousness which is never able to ground itself in some cohesive and comforting sense of reality, despite the frenzy of its hero's efforts.

Emperor and Galilean is an immense dramatic work comprised of two complete plays, *Caesar's Apostasy* and *The Emperor Julian.* However, the drama focuses precisely upon Julian's response to his concept of *empire.* The range of this image is wide and yet it is an intense metaphor. For Julian, the notion of empire objectifies his sense of that which is external to his conscious mind. In the earlier stages of the play, his concept of empire embraces a paradigm of sensual objects and experiences which are forbidden to him. He is divided by conflicting temptations: the promise of a secure and knowable reality which offers him the promise of identity as the instrument of God with a secure place in a divine cosmology and the promise of personal power and sensual satisfaction in the pleasures which could be his as the successor to Constantius, the Emperor of Rome. At the beginning of the drama Ibsen clarifies that Constantinople is a place converted to Christianity in rhetoric only. Christian metaphors are voiced primarily as political strategies, and the actual substance of faith is not brought into play. The dialectic, Emperor and Galilean, is not the basic conflict of the play. Empire and Christianity are in themselves metaphors projecting two differing concepts of the relationship between the individual consciousness and the reality of its environment, and both are mythical. Empire, to Julian, eventually comes to mean the absolute identification of the self with power, encompassing within his own consciousness the energy of the world, making his will the source of each tangible manifestation of reality. The Christian myth, to Julian, is the sense of his being the instrument of power, not its source. Each mythical construct of reality is an escape from the phenomenal experience he fears, although in the beginning of the drama his sense of empire is itself specifically identified with the sensual.

The whole being of the Emperor Constantius is torn by guilt. He is caught in the tension between the desire for power and the fear that within the Christian reality he will be punished for the crimes which that exploitation of power has demanded. Constantius has murdered the family of Julian and Gallos, an act which seems to be the primary source of his guilt and the reason for his acute fear of Gallos and Julian. Empire itself, secular power, seems to be the source of sin. Julian fears the temptation of imperial power, and this fear seems to be a major element of his motive to leave Constantinople. His movement to Athens is seen as an escape into the sanctuary of a life which does not threaten with the temptation of power. Initially, the concept of man as an instrument of God's will offers an escape from the temptation to realize personal power within the individual consciousness, and Julian opposes the light of his Christian past with the darkness and fetid air of his present, a present which includes the lure of power:

> I cannot endure the atmosphere of the palace. I think it is unwholesome here. It is so different from Makellon. Makellon lies high. No other city in Cappadocia lies so high; ah, how the fresh snow-wind from Taurus brushes over it.

Julian makes this statement to Agathon, a boyhood friend who has come to the court from Makellon to communicate a vision which he has experienced. Agathon's clearly sincere faith contrasts with Julian's troubled and equivocal declarations; however, the destructive vengeance of Agathon's treatment of the heathen qualifies our response to his use of faith.

Julian and Agathon discuss a church which both Gallos and Julian worked upon in Cappadocia, a structure built over the Holy Mamas's grave. Julian grieves because he was unable to finish his part of the structure, although Gallos completed his. Agathon informs him that the building has stopped: "The builders said it was impossible as you had conceived it." Here is an early image which suggests the attempt to create a structure, a tangible realization of form, which is impossible to fulfill. Julian explains that failure in his declaration that the Holy Mamas was a false saint. This is the initial example of an act which occurs again and again in *Emperor and Galilean*: the devaluation of the present vision of reality; the establishment of that perspective as false, deluded; and the substitution of a new mythology. Julian, for example, returns to the dream his mother experienced immediately before his birth—that she gave birth to Achilles. Agathon then mentions the vision which he has experienced. This vision came to him after the Christians had punished the heathen in Cappadocia for holding secret meetings in the temple of Cybele by wrathfully burning their homes, destroying their treasures, and sacrificing many lives: "Many perished in the flames; we killed more in the streets as they fled. O, it was a wonderful time for the glory of God!" The prophetic revelation came to him after he experienced an acute despair, suffering fever and raging in an irrational state:

> Before me on the wall was a white shining light, and in the rays of the light stood a man in a floor-length cape. Rays of light shone out from his head; he held a reed in his hand and fastened his eyes gently upon me. . . . And then he spoke and said: "Stand up, Agathon; search for him who shall inherit the kingdom; bid him to go into the lions' lair and fight with them!"

Julian sees this vision as an allegory in which the lions represent the pagan philosophers, but Agathon continues: "Announce to the elect that he shall shake the dust of the imperial city from his feet, and never again enter its gates." This vision, then, is able to function as a mythology which justifies Julian's retreat from Constantinople, his escape from the experience he fears.

At this point Gallos appears, shaken by his summons

to the Emperor. He identifies Constantius as the murderer of his family and accuses Julian of being his present betrayer. His identification of the Emperor as his family's assassin and his own fear work to continue the association of fear and guilt with empire, the disease and the perversity of power.

Gallos himself is deceived by Constantius; and when the Emperor appears he appoints Gallos as Caesar, his heir, and dispels the rumors that Julian is to be appointed his successor. Julian sees this escape from the temptation of empire as a blessing. He also learns that Libanius has been exiled—that Rome has been purged of this source of his fear. However, he has been tempted by Libanius, by another form of paganism (the power of the intellect) which attacks his ego, and he uses the mythology of Agathon's vision to justify his escape from home.

PRINCE JULIAN.   And in the morning, my Agathon, in the morning to Athens!
AGATHON.   To Athens? You are to go to Pergamos.
PRINCE JULIAN.   Hush! You do not understand— we must be as sly as serpents. First to Pergamos— and then to Athens!

That lightly used metaphor, "sly as serpents," reveals that Julian's act, his justification of his action in terms of an apparently Christian vision, is just the opposite; it marks his identification with the demonic. In the poetic structure of the play, light and dark play a significant part in the clarification of the conflict between the conscious self and internal and external energies. Initially the metaphor of salvation—in Christian terms, the union of the will of the individual with the will of God—is projected in images of light: Julian is the source of light for Agathon whom he converted to belief; Makellon is in the heights, touched by light. Yet the temptation which comes to Julian is clarified itself in the promise of his own "shin[ing] forth over the empire." And there is a confusion between the pagan and the Christian as the source of light for Julian. The conflict between Christianity and empire in *Emperor and Galilean* is not a simple one, in any sense. This individual tension between a sense of will as the self and a sense of will as divine power external to consciousness is the issue; and empire extends its meaning to include the manifestation of personal authority and power, wisdom, and the enjoyment of sensuality.

Early in the play it is obvious that Julian himself fears that he will lose his faith; he is tempted by the glorification of individual consciousness which is implicit in the intellectual celebrations of the philosophers. He fears, as well, that he will be chosen as Caesar and will have the range of personal power implicit in that election. Eventually, of course, empire and the lure of philosophy (man or ego-centered power) become part of the same model; but at the early movement of the play they remain somewhat distinct. Libanius confronts Julian with the temptations of pagan philosophy, stressing its sensual pleasures within an appealing image of form:

> A whole beautiful world exists to which you Galileans are blind. Within it, existence is a solemn occasion among statues, with singing in the temple, and with full bowls foaming over, and roses in our hair. Enormous bridges span the distance from one spirit to another to the end of light and space.
>
> I know one who could be the ruler over this vast sunlit empire.

When Julian replies that such kingship would mean losing the chance of salvation, Libanius replies: "What is salvation? Reunion with the primal source . . . Reunion like the raindrop with the sea, like the mouldering leaf with the earth which nurtured it." Here is the sense that the Christian concept of reconciliation with the divine is a loss of identity, a giving up of the self to an energy external to it. It is the submission of will, not the realization of it. The image of the sea as the primal source is of crucial importance here. In the Ibsen canon no single metaphor resounds as deeply as the image of the sea—

clarifying as it does the lure of freedom, the threat of death, the illusion of the self-determined self, the regressive retreat into an illusion of freedom, and the reality of self-destruction. Later Julian cries: "I feel like Daedalus, between sky and sea. A terrifying height and an abysmal depth."

The primary condition of Julian's imagination is his anxiety as he faces the obscurity of his perception of the universe and the source of power. This confusion, seen in the image of suspension between the depths and the heights, is significant. Like Daedalus, Julian sees the gaining of the heavens as a possibility on the basis of his own energy, his own assertion. But the fate of Daedalus is known, the plunge to the depths—the obscure and unknown. Julian's desire voices itself in the demand *to know*, to comprehend. To know is to possess in Julian's sense, and it is the unknown which terrifies and yet lures, because the substance of the unknown offers the possibility of being embraced in knowledge. The tension between the known and the unknown is more fully explored in the spatial metaphor which I quoted in the introduction:

Do you know the way in which I became filled with spiritual perception?—It happened during a night of prayer and fasting. I sensed that I was pulled far away —far away into space and out of time; for I was surrounded by full, sun-streaming day, and I stood alone on a ship with slack sails in the middle of the glassy, shining, Greek sea. Islands towered high, like pale, congealed banks of clouds, far away, and the ship lay heavily as if it slept on the middle of the wind-blue plain.

Listen, this plain then became more and more transparent, lighter, thinner, until finally it was no more, and my ship hung over a terrible, empty depth. No growth, no sunlight down there—only the bottom of the sea, dead, slimy, black in all its loathsome nakedness.

But above in that infinite arch which before had seemed empty to me, there was life; there invisibility assumed form, and silence became sound.

A sense of the impenetrable mystery of the depths of the sea—dark, formless, threatening, revealed as filthy and slimy in its nakedness—is implicit in this image of the ship suspended between the heavens and the abyss of the sea. To know the abyss is to see it as revolting. Arched over the abyss are the comprehensible heavens which have form and order. Julian's vision suggests the conflict in his own imagination between what is consciously organized and structured (what he himself can order) and the mysterious chaos of the abyss. Also there is that typical act of Julian's imagination present in the dream: the evasion of the present reality by the creation of a new concept of reality—"That which is, is not; and that which is not, is." The desire to form reality within consciousness, avoiding the threat of dealing with a reality external to the conscious mind, is a major force in Julian's consciousness.

The first chapter discussed the action of *Brand* in terms of the creation of myths of order in the consciousness of its hero. The second chapter examined *Peer Gynt's* use of the transitions in consciousness between the phenomenal and the illusory. This action is even clearer in *Emperor and Galilean* since the primary and explicit content of the play is the creation and dissolution in Julian's imagination of concepts of reality in which he is the center. The pattern repeats itself: the ecstatic affirmation of a reality and the embittered disillusion when that sense of reality fails.

Agathon refuses to go with Julian to Athens with Libanius who is, in Julian's rhetoric, the primary lion with whom he is "chosen" to do battle. Act 1 ends with Julian's commitment to a new mythology, or rather, a reinterpreted one: "They are weighing anchor. Good winds, winged lion; Achilles follows in your wake. . . . Ah, there falls a star." His identification with the combined prophecies of Agathon and his mother is clarified, not as the unfoldment of a cosmic promise, but as the creation of his own imagination.

Act 2 reveals Julian's disillusionment with Libanius— sickened by his greed, political exploitation, egotism. His despair continues and his investigations of the Eleusian mysteries is a new exploration of the problem of identity. When Gregory confronts him with the obvious evil of Gallos's reign as Caesar, Julian retreats from an assertion which would enact his faith in the Christian scheme of reality. Ibsen poses this retreat in the image of an inability to confront the nature of the abyss—one quality of which is Julian's own latent desire for power, his feared desire to possess. Gregory describes the evil present in Antioch:

> The unheard-of outrage has come down upon Antioch like a plague. All evil awakes and swarms up from its hiding place. My mother writes that it is as if a reeking abyss had opened up. Wives inform on their husbands, sons inform on their fathers, priests on the members of their own congregation—!

When it is revealed to Julian that the empire of his brother is rank, sensual, and destructive, the complexities of the image of empire grow. Ibsen uses the metaphor of the abyss to contain the sense of a violent, destructive, irrationality. Immediately after Gregory reads this letter from his mother in Cappadocia, Julian witnesses a scene of bacchanalian license and sensuality; and he ignores the painful truth of his brother's sin and his own responsibility in directing his attention to the lustful spectacle:

PRINCE JULIAN.   Ah, look at him whom they are driving naked among them. Now the dancing-girls. Ah, see what—

BASILIOS OF CESAREA.   Fie, fie; turn your eyes away! . . .

PRINCE JULIAN (*after a brief silence*).   Tell me, Basilios, why is the heathen sin so beautiful?

After this incident, Julian questions Basilios about his sister Makrina, whose Christian asceticism seems to hold a kind of appeal for Julian. It is very significant that the image of Makrina is introduced here. This woman is dedicated to an ascetic life—a continued sexual innocence. Julian's imagination fastens on her as he moves away from a confrontation with both the temptations and the responsibility of empire. Gallos is clearly a vengeful and destructive tyrant and, within the distribution of qualities in the play, an image of virile sexuality. His love for Helena was suggested early in the play. Within *Emperor and Galilean*, there is an association of sexuality and an aggressive oppression of people. Makrina is the antithesis of sexuality and aggression. Julian seems attracted to her because of her innocence and her ability to renounce the world.

PRINCE JULIAN.   When you read to me from her letters, it is as though I perceived something whole and full which I have desired for a long time. Tell me, is she still firmly resolved to turn away from the world and live in a deserted region?

BASILIOS OF CESAREA.   She has kept that resolution.

PRINCE JULIAN.   Truly? She on whom all valued gifts have been bestowed. She who is supposed to be both young and beautiful; she who has wealth in prospect and possesses—how rare for a woman— exceptionally fine learning! What will she do in solitude?

BASILIOS OF CESAREA.   I have told you her fiancé died. She considers him to be her intended bridegroom, to whom she devotes every thought and whom she feels obligated to meet in purity.

Later Julian sees Makrina as "the pure woman" with whom he might, in his own divinity, found a new generation of mankind. In his imagination Makrina is the object of his desire; but it is her conscious innocence which makes her attractive to him. The "pure" is crucial. Makrina is the prototype of the critical female figure in Ibsen's drama: the beautiful woman who is not allowed to commit herself to the process of sexuality. Her desirability is dependent upon her innocence, and the maintenance of that innocence is the reason for the renunciation of the hero. Makrina is related to Solveig and is the model for Hedwig, Rebekka, and Irene. In Ibsen, one aspect of the hero's suffering is his asceticism. A major element of his alienation from nature is his inability to have a natural sexual relationship. The typical Ibsenian hero is either damaged emotionally or, if that is not the case, he makes some kind of renunciation which denies sexuality. In this case, the sacrifice is seen as necessary to free the soul from earthly commitments, in order to create the world of the imagination, the formal product, the realization of the individual will.

Helena functions as the image of eroticism antithetical to Makrina's renunciation. The clear antipathy toward sexuality in *Emperor and Galilean* voices itself in the image of this sensual woman who dies in delirium, poisoned by fruit sent from her brother, the Emperor Constantius. Her frenzied confession reveals her erotic love for Gallos, her hatred and disgust for Julian, and the fact that she has accepted a priest as a lover in the illusion of being loved by Jesus:

> Are you angry with me, glorious one? Gallos is dead. Beheaded. What a blow that must have been. Do not be jealous my first and last. Burn Gallos in the flames of hell: it was always you, you, you! I will not see him after this. You know our sweet secret. You, my day's desire, my night's ecstasy! It was you yourself—in the form of your servant—in the antechamber; yes, yes, you were there; it was you, in the darkness, in the air, in the thick clouds of frankincense, that night when the unborn Caesar growing under my heart—

Julian responds to his discovery of Helena's sexuality with the cry—"Abyss of all abysses," clarifying even more directly the relationhip between sexuality and the meta-

phor of the abyss. The eroticism which is the reality of
Helena's nature is only thinly disguised within the illusion of Christian faith. When it releases itself, it releases
itself in a fantasy in which the erotic takes the form of
the sacred, and the ecstasy of sexuality equates with the
ecstasy of ritualistic communion. In a sense, Helena's
action is a parallel to Julian's, and yet it is the negative
of that act. Helena's act is to confront the abyss—her
own sexuality—and to transform it in her imagination
into the form of an act of faith—the union with Christ.
Julian retreats from his own sexuality and transforms
that retreat, first into the form of faith and then into the
form of paganism, identifying his control with asceticism.

Julian's search for a new reality manifests itself in a
rejection of each formulated or fixed doctrine, and in his
anxiety he returns to that crucial image of the ship suspended between the abyss and the heavens:

> Do you not feel disgust and nausea as if you were
> aboard a ship in a calm, tossed between life and the
> word, heathen wisdom and beauty. There must be a
> new revelation. Or a revelation of something new.
> There *must*, I say; the time has come. Yes, a revela-
> tion! O, Basilios, if you could only pray that to come
> over me! A martyr's death, if it must be—! A martyr's
> death—ah, its sweetness makes me dizzy, a crown of
> thorns around my temples—! (*He grasps his head with
> both hands and seizes the crown of roses which he rips
> off, thinking to himself for a long while and saying
> softly:*) That. I had forgotten that. (*He casts the
> wreath away.*) There is one thing I have learned in
> Athens. . . . The old beauty is no longer beautiful,
> and the new truth is no longer true.

Julian's inability to gain a stable sense of identity in
either world, the pagan or the Christian, is focused in his
desire to fix his identity in the security of a martyr's
death: an act in which the rigidity of the doctrine—the
stasis of the boundless arch of heaven—would not be sub-

ject to the law of change. Julian's fear of change then manifests itself in his sense of the possibility of a new vision of reality to be gained from Maximus.

Julian's vision of the third empire is an attempt to reconcile the conflicting desires of heaven and the abyss. Maximus defines the three empires as Christian, pagan, and the third realm which is a synthesis of the two notions of reality. The metaphor which unifies the Christian and pagan myths of reality is the image of an innocent woman. The metaphor of the innocent woman is critically significant: this image is related to the temptations of the abyss; and yet in the freedom from guilt—and the suggestion of no change—this image is related to the fixed arch of heaven. This image presents the temptation of sexuality without the threat. The quality of Julian's vision is certainly determined by the manipulation of Maximus, and we cannot accept this perception as real. However, Julian's response to these images projects the quality of his own vision of reality.

The representatives of the two empires in Julian's vision are Cain and Judas, each instrumental in the dissolution of the primary state of that empire or reality. Julian's identification, then, is with an agent of what we could call some kind of *negative power*; his identification is also with figures who have imagined that they are enacting their own will but who, on the contrary, have enacted a divinely projected plan within Christian mythology. The primary realization of Julian's consciousness, which he consistently rejects and yet must return to, is the recognition that the nature of will itself is illusory—that each is subject to some external energy, characterized as Necessity or God: ". . . I willed . . . what I must." Maximus himself identifies Julian as the founder of the third empire, declaring that he is the "third great liberated man under necessity." Julian refuses the claim initially, shouting: "I defy necessity! I will not serve it! I am free, free, free!" However, Julian immediately learns that Gallos is dead, and that he is designated Caesar, fulfilling the vision of Apollinaris.

Julian then chooses to fulfill another myth, succumbing this time to the temptation of empire, the myth of individual will. Each of Julian's choices is clearly defined by Ibsen as the enactment of a vision or the fulfillment of some mythical conception of reality. Julian consistently works to transcend the present reality by endeavoring to realize an image of himself which is defined externally. This image is always a means to escape or to ignore the present reality which threatens him. At the conclusion of this third act, Julian accepts the temptation of empire; he sees the power of empire as a means of encompassing that which is external—the ability to possess the object of desire. Empire is the choice of phenomenal experience seen as the choice of form.

Ibsen's work makes the difficult but necessary distinction between the will as conscious determination and the acceptance of the self as some kind of complex totality. The vulnerability of the self to an external force is acutely feared by Ibsen's characters. A strong and compelling fear voices itself throughout the play that the hero's life is not the consequence of his will but is, on the contrary, the inevitable working out of some externally developed processes. In the complex image of empire, Julian attempts to see himself free from God, an agent in himself, rather than an instrument or a vessel for energies located elsewhere. And yet it is clear within this play that the concept of self-determined, consciously derived action is a fiction indulged in by the hero. Julian's myth of the will is precisely that, an imaginative construct in which he views himself as self-determining. In his use of the occult Julian sees the existence of some kind of mysterious power, and yet he feels that he can use that power. He thinks that spiritualism can become his instrument. In a strange ambiguity he sees himself as willed to be a hero. In an equivocal vision Julian sees that he is willed to be self-determining, and he interprets the declaration "I willed . . . what I must" as an imperative to act out his own desires.

Emperor and Galilean explores a critical psychic

problem: the relation of the self and the other—or, perhaps in clearer terms, the relationship of the self and the object. One aspect of this exploration is the imitation of Julian's creation of successive myths of possession, the construction of illusions in which he enacts patterns of domination of those forces he encounters. The basic tension of the drama is not a conflict between Christianity and paganism, but rather between man and nature, between man's sense of his own being and those forces which would work upon that being—changing, injuring, and eventually destroying the finely wrought and treasured image of the self both in a physical and a metaphysical sense.

The conflict between concepts of selfhood defined internally and concepts of selfhood defined externally is consistently present in the play. Julian is the victim of a series of mythologies which he feels compelled to enact; he is dependent upon a mythology for a sense of identity and purpose. This need is analogous to Brand's dependence upon the form or order of the myth of the absolute will. Here, however, the plays differ significantly: Julian suffers a series of disillusionments rather than the final, single destructive recognition which Brand experiences in the Ice Church. Both Brand's single mythology and Julian's series of mythologies are attempts to avoid confrontation with the nature of phenomenal experience.

The visions which are presented to Julian are interpreted by him, usually, and they are used by him to justify his desires—latent or conscious. However, he does need and demand external justification and affirmation. At the end of the first play Julian must make the choice between following the action which would be defined by his Christian belief or proceeding with the action necessary to assume the identity of emperor. Ibsen dramatizes this choice in a highly theatrical scene which concludes the final act of this portion of the double drama.

Julian, sequestered in the catacombs of a great church

in Vienna, manifests his choice by descending into the lower reaches of this place to offer pagan sacrifice. He does this in counterpoint to the choral repetition of the *pater noster* heard from the cathedral above him. In one sense, the presentation of this prayer—"Lead us not into temptation, but deliver us from evil"—acts as a warning to Julian. It also functions as a means of presenting Julian's identification with deity: "Free, free! Mine is the kingdom!" And the play ends with the invocation: "forever and ever. Amen," clarifying that Julian's desire is for a timelessness, a stopping of process, the infinite stasis of form.

The second play of the pair of plays which comprises *Emperor and Galilean, The Emperor Julian,* is considerably less interesting and less powerful than the first. The final section of this epic drama is less energetic and varied in its language and, unfortunately, does not develop the paradoxes established in the earlier play with any more depth and intensity. It does, however, focus upon Julian's increasing identification with a mythical concept of his own being.

Julian's assumption of the empire marks his complete break with the faith of the Galilean, and he reinstitutes pagan worship, returning to the traditional forms of ritual and worship. However, his acceptance of the pagan practices is uneasy and anxious because he still fears sexual experience. He seems to experience a revulsion at sensational, physical experience. After leading a Dionysian procession, he returns to his palace revolted:

> Was there beauty in this? Where were the old men with their white beards? Where were the innocent young girls with bands on their foreheads, with fine jewel boxes, modest even in the pleasure of the dance?
>
> For shame, you whores! (*He tears off his panther-skin and casts it to one side.*)
>
> Where has beauty gone? Can not the Emperor bid it to come again and have it come?
>
> Damn all this stinking fornication!

> What faces? Every vice cries out from these dis-
> tracted features. Abcessed bodies and souls.
> Fy, fy! A bath, Agilo! The stench suffocates me.
> . . . The bath? No, let that be. What is the filth of
> the body compared with all the rest?

The play builds upon an explicit progress through
each of the three empires—the Christian, the pagan,
and the synthetic empire with Julian as godhead; however, in that obvious structural sequence the clear antithesis of the physical and material worlds is implicit.
Julian's paganism, as described earlier, is ascetic and
does not focus upon the pleasures of the senses but
rather dedicates itself to worship, ritual, sacrifice, intellectual activity—much to the displeasure of his subjects
and his court. However, his denial of Christianity is
manifested in violence and sensuality. Ibsen never embodies the pagan in sensual delight and ecstasy but
rather voices it in metaphors of revulsion or images of
violence and painful injury:

> In the midst of an obscene feast of Aphrodite, the
> heathens broke into the house of our holy sisters,
> violated them, murdered them with unspeakable
> tortures. . . . Some of the wretches even ripped open
> the bodies of the martyrs, pulled out the intestines
> and ate the liver raw!

Julian's enactment of myth completes itself in his
sense of his own deity. It is important that this movement begins as a political, rhetorical strategy and eventually fulfills itself in Julian's own delusion—his own
identification with God in the sense that his immortal
being has encompassed the being of Christ himself in
some kind of evolution of deity. He puts forward a
dream whose basic strategy seems to be his identification with the divine:

> I dreamed that before my eyes I saw a child who
> was followed by a rich man who owned countless
> flocks but who despised the worship of the gods.

This evil man annihilated the child's entire family. But Zeus took pity upon the child itself, and he held his hand over him.

Thereupon I saw that child grow up into a young man under the care of Minerva and Apollo.

I dreamed further that the young man fell asleep upon a stone under the open heavens.

Then Hermes stepped down upon the ground in the form of a young man and said: "Come; I will show you the way which will lead you to the dwelling of the highest god!"—So he led the youth to the foot of a very steep mountain. There he left him.

The youth burst out weeping, moaning, and cried out to Zeus with a loud voice. Behold, Minerva and the Sun King, who rules over the whole earth, then stepped close to him, lifted him up to the mountain peak, pointed out and revealed to him his family's inheritance.

But this inheritance was the expanse of the earth, from sea to sea, and beyond the seas.

This speech is clearly a rhetorical passage, deliberately planned by Julian to persuade his army and advisors of his divinity; however, it also reveals the way the metaphor of empire works in his consciousness. Julian's dream of authority is seen in the image of vision from the heights. This vision is an image of comprehension in that reality can be seen, identified; and it is an image of encompassing or possessing in a distant and abstract way. Implicit in the image of the vision from the heights is the sense of removal or withdrawal from that world which is seen. The ambiguity is acute because while the sense of possession is very strong, it is balanced by a sense of remoteness and distance. The possession of that reality is an experience within consciousness, abstract and apart from phenomenal experience. Within this dream his personal nature is exceptional; he is the lost child who is found and raised by the gods. His inheritance is displayed to him by Zeus, the prime deity. In this vision Julian is not only the possessor of all of the reality held within his sight, but he is himself the focus of the attention of the gods. His being reaches out and encompasses the desired object and yet remains the focus of desire and attention from other beings.

In increasing desperation and frenzy Julian sees himself as divine, including and surpassing the being of Jesus, the Galilean. The vision given him by Maximus provides an image of himself as the agent for the transfiguration of the world, uniting the pagan and spiritual, encompassing the being of the Galilean and his own unique identity. However, within this scheme the unresolvable dialectic continues to divide Julian's consciousness: the identification with the world, with sensual experience, and the desire to renounce that world, to move away from phenomenal experience.

In the following scene Julian meets Makrina for the first time, seeing the woman who has been the symbol of renunciation and perfect innocence. She sees her life of renunciation destroyed by him. She is appalled and attracted by Julian and voices that ambivalence in a speech which discloses her own tension between the sensual and the ascetic: "Woe is me that I ever saw these shining eyes! Angel and serpent in one being; the apostate's desire and the tempter's cunning together!" This image describes the antithesis of the mythical and phenomenal, the dialectic of two forces within Julian's consciousness. The empire seems to offer Julian the satisfactions of phenomenal experience, but Julian uses his secular power not to identify himself with sensuality but rather as a strategy for renouncing sensual pleasure. He uses the concept of empire to create a myth which removes him as far as possible from the phenomenal and establishes him free from the processes of time.

Julian does not desire knowledge in the simple sense of a clear, unobstructed vision of reality. He wishes to comprehend his universe and to be able to order it within his own mind. Increasingly he seems to want the world to be the emanation of his own consciousness; he wants his total experience—the complete ambiance of his action—to be the manifestation of his will. He wants to be the object which is cared for and adored by the world. He wants to be the focal point, not the origin, of the action; this desire is the source of Ibsen's paradox. This paradox is embodied in the play in Julian's movement from identification with the heroic to identification with God himself. The action of *Emperor and Galilean* is the dissolution of the illusion of comprehension. The recognition of the illusory nature of each myth projected in this drama is not the cause of a realistic confrontation with the nature of the universe in any existential sense; rather, each disillusionment is the occasion for a reformation of an operative myth.

The resolution of the play does not confirm either the rationality or irrationality of the world. It does work toward the assumption that the nature of the universe cannot be comprehended and that individual will has no integrity or unique determination, but is—in all probability—the instrument of some rational or irrational will. The revelation of the play is that the concept of a determining will within the consciousness of man is, in itself, a myth; but that the formation of myth is a process which is integrally involved in man's response to the irrationality of his own being.

Ironically, Julian is killed by Agathon, the young man whom he converted to Christianity during their childhood in Cappadocia. Agathon describes their relationship in the early part of the play as the embodiment of innocence, conceived in images of light and purity: "Was not God strong in you [Julian] when you led me out of the darkness of heathendom, and gave me light for all time—you, a child as you were then!" Julian considers that time as a dream, sadly lost: "That should be so now! Where did I find the words of fire? There were songs of praise in the air. There was a ladder between heaven and earth—." Julian's hysterical identification with the energies of the universe and Agathon's fanatical demand to kill him as the anti-Christ are related. Ironically, Agathon is the product of Julian's childhood Christianity. Also, the violence and fury of Agathon's faith is clarified in that initial scene as he describes the wrathful vengence the Christians have used upon the heathen. Agathon's killing of Julian also fulfills Julian's own vision of how he will be killed. Julian sees hosts of Galileans in the sky where Anatolus sees a clustering of clouds as the light of day begins:

> Look—they in the clothes edged in red, they are those who suffered martyrs' deaths. Singing women surround them and spin bowstrings of long hair torn from their heads. Children are in their company, —twining slings from their unfastened intestines. Burning torches! There, a thousandfold! —countless! They rush toward here. They all are looking at me; they all are coming right toward me!

This metaphor of resurrected children suggests that strange image of the awakened dead troll children in *Brand*, a metaphor which embodied Brand's guilt and his fear of process. This image in *Emperor and Galilean* is Julian's projection of his own response to himself as the cruel persecutor of the Christians, his own guilt at the suffering and destruction his mythical identification has caused. It is also an acute image of the strength of the Galileans, his own fear of their retribution, their vengeful and aggressive energies directed toward him. The vision also contains the significant transformation of the static and calm spatial image of the heavens. The "infinite arch of heaven" has been the insistent metaphor of form in *Emperor and Galilean*, and here it is transformed into an image of the abyss. In *Brand* the resurrection of the demonic children took place in the depths; that resurrection in *Emperor and Galilean* takes place in the heavens which then assume the nature of the demonic. The movement of this metaphor is related to the image of form in *Brand*, the Ice Church, transformed into the abyss. Julian's fatal injury is made by the spear which wounded Christ at Golgotha, and

Julian's wound is also in the side. In this limited sense, Julian does enact mythical identification with Christ although the resolution of *Emperor and Galilean* works more toward the sense of the failure of Julian's mythical identification. Julian, of course, sees himself in the typical movement from darkness into light. His consciousness has consistently attempted to move from obscurity to comprehension although his concepts of an understandable reality have been increasingly illusory. His death is seen by him in images of failing light. He does make a final effort to identify himself with Alexander: "(*with closed eyes.*) To Alexander was given his entry— into Babylon. —I will also —Beautiful laurel wreathed youths —dancing maidens, but so far away. Beautiful earth, —beautiful earth life—." However, his final affirmation of his reality is made with open eyes: "Oh, sun, sun, —why do you betray me?"

The use of *sol* [sun] in this final moment is an image which focuses all that is included in Julian's sense of light—innocence, comprehension, freedom, vitality. He sees his movement toward the light as a deception. Again, Ibsen projects the failure of the mythical. In his final campaign Julian forces Makrina to accompany his forces, tending to the sick. She cares for him as well, and after he dies she interprets his death as a divine strategy. With Basilios, Makrina is the source for the perpetuation of the mythical.

BASILIOS OF CESAREA. I sense so clearly that here lies a glorious, shattered instrument of God.

MAKRINA. Yes, truly, a dear and priceless instrument.

BASILIOS OF CESAREA. Christ, Christ, why is it that your people did not see your self-evident teachings? The Emperor Julian was a chastizing rod, not toward death, but toward resurrection. . . . is it not written: "there are formed vessels for honor and vessels for dishonor."

MAKRINA. O, Brother, let us not attempt to think

to the bottom of that abyss. (*She leans over the corpse and covers its face.*) Sinning soul of man, if you were *forced* to sin, good shall certainly be bestowed upon you on that magnificent day when the Mighty appears in the sky to speak judgment over the living dead and the dead who live!

The myth cannot remain in an unequivocal state. The act of the drama has been the disintegration of the mythical, and yet the impetus toward the formal remains in force, held by those who have renounced the processes of sexual experience, whose asceticism is an attempt to preserve their own realization of form.

4

The Wild Duck

The ten years (1873 to 1883) between the completion of *Emperor and Galilean* and his initial work on *The Wild Duck* were a continuation of Ibsen's exile. He moved from Dresden to Munich, from Munich to Rome, and from Rome back to Munich. During this time Ibsen was at work exploring and experimenting with a dramatic form which was to result in his international reputation as the leading figure in the movement of dramatic realism. Ibsen concentrated upon figures of ordinary men and women in moments of family and community crisis in *Pillars of Society* (1877), *A Doll's House* (1879), and *An Enemy of the People* (1882). The particular style which we identify as Ibsen's becomes clear in these plays. The primary determinant of this style is the internal pressure and density of the play which is the result of an image of a mythic vision, the recurrent drama of consciousness, being contained in a domestic environment within the plausible dreams and anxieties of these ordinary figures. Through the strict control of providing psychological motivation and a sense of plausibility for each primary metaphor, the text becomes a resonant and multilayered object. In these realistic works each use of the images drawn from the spatial metaphor which was freely and openly used in *Brand*, *Peer Gynt*, and *Emperor and Galilean* has a restrained energy which allows it to operate on the realistic level and yet lead our imaginations toward the more essential drama existing beneath the surface of its more commonplace displacement. Despite the mechanical conversion of Bernick at the resolution of *Pillars of Society*, the feared image of Olaf's death in the rotten vessel which Bernick would allow to be put to sea suggests a metaphor of guilt, bringing together the basic images of the processes of decay, the abyss, and the dead child in *Brand*. The tension in this play between a projected quality of virtuous being and a reality of exploitation, lust, and deceit is artificially resolved but interestingly explored. In *A Doll's House* there is a strong sense of the movement through the illusory toward the real, although within the ambiguity of this play, Nora's recognition of the nature of reality is only partially a positive act. Her act is also a movement toward a more complex, difficult, and hostile reality which includes the irrationality of her own being. The recurrent tension between a desire for innocence and an acute sense of guilt is clear in *Ghosts*, and it is not difficult to see the action as the ironic dissolution of a myth of possible innocence accomplished by the intrusion of phenomenal reality into that dream, the recognition of the destructive processes of sexuality. In *An Enemy of the People*, Ibsen seems to intensify his characterization of general humanity as selfish and exploitative in a drama which once more puts forward a concept of a willed movement toward the pure, free, and self-determined as vulnerable to energies of an irrational and hostile human nature.

In a study such as this one the selection of plays closely examined must be limited. It seems to me that *The Wild Duck* is the most logical choice from the group of those works generally classified in the middle realistic period. In this play the antithetical pressures of the playwright's demand to be plausible and the demand of his personal metaphors which were so much a part of his imaginative processes meet to produce a work which is simultaneously a brilliantly realistic and a profoundly poetic work. In dramas as obviously formal as *Brand*, *Peer Gynt*, and *Emperor and Galilean*, there is a freedom in the language to carry a level of metaphor without providing a consistently intricate and integral relationship between the consciousness of each character and the quality of his imagery. In these less realistic dramas metaphor can be functional without necessarily being designed to illuminate character. In *The Wild Duck*, however, as in most realistic dramas, the primary movement of the play is the gradual revelation of that which is clouded, disguised, and hidden—the coming to the surface of the latent identities of its characters, obscured by their efforts to create illusions of identity. The quality of the dreams and anxieties which define their latent identities is communicated to us through the images which these tensions call up. The collective metaphoric models they construct suggest the basic act of consciousness which Ibsen himself was putting into play. In this sense, the metaphoric structure of a play such as *The Wild Duck* is much more complex than the analogous use of language in a play such as *Brand*.

On September 2, 1884, Ibsen wrote a letter to his publisher, Fredrik Hegel which included the following statement:

> In some ways this new play occupies a position by itself among my dramatic works, its plan and method differing in several respects from my former ones. . . . I also think that *The Wild Duck* may perhaps entice some of our young dramatists into new paths, which I think is desirable.[1]

It is clear that Ibsen saw *The Wild Duck* as innovative, and it is necessary for us to deal both with the uniqueness and the typicality of this play. The sense of the past intruding itself upon the future relates *The Wild Duck* to *Ghosts*, and both plays share the recognition of a young girl's parentage as a crucial and telling event. The two plays, as well, share a consideration of the destructive aspect of public opinion when reputation is held up as the primary value. Despite these similarities, however, there is a critical difference in *The Wild*

Duck. And yet that difference is not easy to isolate in a critical discussion.

In *Ghosts*, the temporal structure remains conventional. The action is the clarification of reality, the sudden disintegration of an illusion and the revelation of a malignant and sordid presence. In this play the disclosures are made to Manders, Oswald, and Regina by Mrs. Alving when she decides to dissolve the myth of Captain Alving which she has created. The relationship of Oswald and Mrs. Alving is telling. She has fed Oswald's imagination with a false picture of Captain Alving to keep the threatening evil of this man from his son. In order to do this she has removed Oswald from his home, denying him the normal relationship of mother and son. Oswald has developed away from home in some freer environment. His return is to a place described in images of darkness, gloom, restriction, oppression, unhappiness, dampness, and cold. His apparent freedom, naturalness, and spontaneity is a model of happiness for his mother. Oswald functions as a symbol of Mrs. Alving's desire and hope; to her, his life seems to be the free assertion and natural condition which she was unable to elect because of her own fear. Her use of Alving money to establish the orphanage is an attempt to solidify the myth of the virtuous father, on one hand, and to cut Oswald free from his father on another, by spending that which belonged to the father. The burning of the orphanage is a complex metaphor: the destruction of the mythical Captain Alving and the re-creation of his consuming presence which destroys Oswald from within. The identity of Alving returns to his wife in the aggressive eroticism of his son. All the fearful taboos come back into play; and, as his mother, she even sees herself capable of providing for him an incestuous relationship with Regina. Oswald becomes the seat of malignancy, losing that very freedom of which he is the symbol, becoming her hopeless child crying for death. Mrs. Alving has attempted to create a myth of innocence centered on Oswald, seeing him as the product of her own renunciation; and yet she is unable to stay the processes of sexuality seen in the form of inherited disease. Oswald is the dead child whose function moves from being the promise of a new race to an image of guilt; as such, he is related to the figure of Alf in *Brand* and Helena's unborn child in *Emperor and Galilean*. He is also the child who is renounced in order to maintain the mythical condition of consciousness. At the same time, he is the means of projecting the movement from form to formlessness; in the violence of his disease he is related to the image of the dead Galilean children, twisting their entrails, returning to life to kill Julian. In the return of the son (who is the image of the father) to a condition of helplessness, he is related to Peer in the ending of that play, as the son and surrogate mother achieve an innocent relationship based upon past eroticism which had been denied. Like Julian, Oswald cries for the sun, dying in an illusion that the release of death is the warmth and light of the sun. This image returns us to the ways in which the attempts of Brand and Julian to release themselves from guilt are seen in metaphors of light. But this image of freedom and comfort is, ironically, the vision of a lunatic juxtaposed with the unyielding reality of process, seen in images of darkness, cold, and unending rain, and the organic deterioration of Oswald's own body initiated by the sexuality of his father.

In *The Wild Duck* that sense of an inexorable fate does not voice itself in as focused an image as "the sins of the fathers" but takes form as a vision of reality so hostile that only one figure within the world of the play can confront it without illusion. Perhaps each of Ibsen's heroes prior to this play seeks a form of innocence or emancipation from guilt with some clarity, deliberation, and sense of personal assertion. Surely each suffers the recognition that the condition of innocence toward which he has moved is impossible to achieve; and yet there is some notion that the attempt is a desirable act even if its objective is unobtainable. The process of

revelation in *Ghosts* leads toward Mrs. Alving's acute
horror at the end of the play in which she faces the
hostility of reality without suppression or illusion. In
The Wild Duck reality is as hostile as in *Ghosts,* but
there is no moment of such focused confrontation with
it—not even when the body of Hedvig is carried from the
garret, because Relling's prediction of Hjalmar's use of
grief moves our attention from the immediate encounter
with the child's death to an image of Hjalmar's exploitation of that event to sustain his illusions. In both
Ghosts and *An Enemy of the People* Ibsen provides a
limited sense of the heroic, some suggestion that the
characters around whom our sympathy forms are attempting to deal with reality honestly and energetically.
Some characters in *The Wild Duck* do face the truth,
but that confrontation is neither open nor unsuppressed.
The Wild Duck is a play of illusions, accommodations,
and adaptations in which the injured and deprived create
forms of order and innocence as strategies to avoid confronting the self. While these strategies fail, the play
ends with the unavoidable suggestion that these illusions
will re-form themselves; and the primary recognition of
reality remains the spectator's.

Perhaps *distribution* is one key to the uniqueness of
The Wild Duck. In most of Ibsen's plays, the confrontation between the self and reality, between the hero, his
vocation, and the reality which that vocation attempts
to order is the event upon which the play focuses. In
this play, however, there is no clear hero whose singular
experience provides the base of the action. Gregers's
act is essential, but his is only one part of an interlocking model. Consequently, rather than focusing our
response upon the experience of a single character whose
death or suffering unifies our perspective at the end of
the work in some cohesive act of identification, we look
at the total world of *The Wild Duck*, judge its inhabit-
ants as victims, and bear witness to their suffering.

The functions of the hero are distributed between
Hjalmar Ekdal and Gregers Werle. Gregers is the

typically demanding idealist whose discomforted vision of reality moves to make that reality conform with his idealism, and yet Gregers is not the hero in any conventional sense. He functions rather as the intruding agent so typical of Ibsen, the figure who returns from the past to disclose a repressed or hidden truth. Gregers's own motive for exposing the truth of Hjalmar's family is itself an attempt to escape from reality. In a curious sense, Gregers is attempting to return Hjalmar to an identity which Gregers admired at an earlier time. Indeed, Gregers is attempting to re-create a Hjalmar who existed only in imagination, and his futile attempt is, in this sense, an escape from a confrontation with the self. His attempt to transform Hjalmar's world reveals an inability to deal with his own problems of identity internally. Gregers does envision himself as a kind of instrument of truth which would purify and expiate the sordid nature of reality, transforming the situation in which he enters; but his truth is a clarification of nature as hostile, an illumination of a reality too terrible for its participants to bear, and he uses his actions as an escape from himself.

The unhappy and injured people of *The Wild Duck* form a strange and pathetic community. The nature of that community is revealed perhaps more by their relationship to the grotesque garret which leads off the Ekdals' rooms than by anything else in the play. The most significant aspect of that place in which Hjalmar and old Ekdal keep rabbits, pigeons, and the wild duck is the fact that it is a made place, an artificially created imitation of the woods. The woods up at the Hoidal works is the place of Old Ekdal's youth, the site where he was once a great sportsman and shot nine bears. The garret is a perverted replica of a conception of nature held in the imaginations of Old Ekdal and his son. This attic room forms a symbol which works both as a metaphor for the characters themselves and as an aspect of the metaphoric structure of the play itself. However, as I mentioned earlier, the most critical aspect of this

visual and textual image is the fact that it is the deliberate construction of a substitute environment, an imitation of the lost woods. Old Ekdal and Hjalmar conceive
of the original as the place of freedom and wildness.
Gregers reminds Old Ekdal of his love of the woods—
"the free life in the forests and in the high plateaus
among the birds and beasts—" and of his passion for
that which is wild and free. The antithesis between the
sense of freedom in nature and its implicit threat is
obvious. The woods at Hoidal are clearly used as an
ambiguous image of Ibsen's hostile world: the lure of
freedom and the consuming processes of life. In a typical
way there is a deliberate equivocation in Ibsen's revelation of the past. While Ekdal was Werle's partner and
in charge of the Hoidal works, timber was cut on government land. Apparently Ekdal did not know he was in
error and acted unknowingly as a dupe to Werle's craft,
serving time in prison and losing his lieutenancy. It is
important, however, that he was ruined as a consequence
of his life in the forest. As Old Ekdal repeats throughout
the play, "the woods avenge themselves."

The clear and grotesque irony of the contained,
limited, restricted imitation of the spacious wilderness is
obvious. Yet that imitation wilderness offers its own
temptations, luring both Hjalmar and his father from
their responsibilities. The perversity of this replica comes
in the fact that it is the result of a regressive movement,
an attempt to return to an earlier life, a life which, in
memory at least, was less threatening and difficult. It is
removed from the present world, providing, as it does,
a "sort of world by itself."

The garret is used by Hjalmar and Old Ekdal as an
escape, and it also serves Hedvig. The garret and its
mysterious contents provide her only contact with the
world beyond her immediate family, and the detach-
ment from reality which this garret represents is integrally related to the function of Hedvig herself as a
character in the play. Hedvig is at a particularly critical
moment in her life—the transition from child to woman.

Time is a threatening entity to the victims of Ibsen's world in *The Wild Duck*, but it forms a threat primarily in the imaginative response of the characters to the painful present and the contrast it holds to their regressive fantasies about the past and their ironic dreams about a better future. Time is static in the garret. It has transitions, as Hedvig notes, becoming a different place in the movement from day to night and from season to season. However, since it exists primarily in the imagination of its users, the garret is not subject to the deteriorations of change in the same sense as the real world. The static nature of the garret is clarified in the image of the figured clock which is at a standstill. Hedvig, as well, is fascinated by the old book of engravings, *Harrison's History of London*, which contains an engraving of death and an hourglass, a picture which frightens the child. The curious possessions of the garret are also said to be the deserted property of a sea captain, drowned at sea, known as the "Flying Dutchman." These images of death and the fact that the attic room is the place of Hedvig's suicide associate the regressive retreat into illusion and the fact of death. It is certainly important that Ibsen associated the garret with his frequent image of the sea. In the third act, Hedvig and Gregers speak of this strange and atypical association:

HEDVIG. . . . it sounds so strange to me when other people say the bottom of the sea.

GREGERS. Why? Tell me why.

HEDVIG. No, I will not; because it is so stupid.

GREGERS. No, I'm sure it's not. Tell me now why you smiled.

HEDVIG. It's because—whenever I suddenly—quite quickly—realize what is in there, it always seems to me that the whole room and everything in it should be called "the bottom of the sea." But it's so stupid.

GREGERS. You should not, absolutely not say that.

HEDVIG. Yes, for it is only a garret.

GREGERS (*looking directly at her*).   Are you so sure of
     that?
HEDVIG (*in amazement*).   That it is a garret?
GREGERS.   Yes, are you so certain?

When it was injured, the wild duck dove to the depths
of the sea, tangling itself in the sea grass in a suicidal
action. However, the "incredibly clever dog" retrieved
the maimed creature, and it has accommodated its injury in the comfortable, restricted, contained life of the
garret. And yet that life which is so different from the
wildness and freedom of its past is a kind of death. The
lure of this created environment which gives its inhab-
itants some limited taste of past pleasures is a temptation to withdraw from experience, from life itself. In
Ibsen's drama, it is the fantasy of the sea which presents
itself to Ellida Wangel; it is the temptation of the sea
at storm which Brand crosses to reach the dying man;
and it is the tempting sea which kills the boy, Eyolf, and
the child-woman, Hedvig.

Part of the complexity of the image of the garret is the
fact that this room is both "the bottom of the sea" and
the place where the wild duck lives in comfort after being rescued from the depths. In an important sense, the
garret represents an accommodation of injury, a strategy
for survival in a hostile situation through the development of an illusion of experience rather than a movement into the reality of experience itself. The fact that
Ibsen saw that kind of accommodation as a kind of
death is clear in Old Werle's definition of Ekdal as an
injured duck which will not return to the surface after
his dive to the depths.

> When Ekdal was set free, he was a broken man, be-
> yond help. There are people in the world who dive
> to the bottom as soon as they get a couple of slugs in
> their body, and they never come up again.

In that sense, Ekdal's illusory life in the garret is a retreat into the depths of the sea, a regressive action which

is a retreat from the reality of the present. It is significant that the wild duck must be kept from seeing the sky or sea since that clear vision of her past would destroy the comfort of her present acceptance of injury and attenuated experience.

The landscape which is the specific realization of Ibsen's primary spatial metaphor is the embodiment of a consciousness; it is a landscape of the mind, held in the metaphors of heights and depths, the forests and the sea. Ibsen's scene is not primarily the projection of the consciousness of the protagonist. Rather, the scene which contains this spatial image is the environment in which the hero's consciousness exists; that consciousness is part of the environment, but the hero's unconscious and a sense of what is external to his consciousness also informs the detail of that environment. And it is not a question of specific manifestations of this spatial image functioning metaphorically for the hero. The hero is himself part of a metaphoric process and the relationship of the hero to a particular aspect of the scene is in itself a metaphoric unit. The relationship of Brand to the Ice Church is the metaphoric unit which works to project an image of the self assuming a relationship to certain internal and external temptations.

In *The Wild Duck* the typical spatial metaphor is displaced and distributed to the degree that it is not a clear and obvious visual scheme. The natural world with its clearly seen heights and depths is largely external to *The Wild Duck*. The scene is internal—not only in the sense of the restricted, contained, unnatural environment of those rooms; but it is internal in the sense that it is withdrawn from that scene in which the basic tensions can be confronted more directly. The basic images are themselves attenuated; and while the work deals with the same tension between the mythical and phenomenal as opposing strategies of consciousness, the reduction of these characters is shown in the attenuation of the mythical quality of the environment. The mythical movements within their consciousnesses voice themselves in images which are smaller, less extraordinary, and within the limitations of their own imaginative grasp. These individual images have resonance but, quite frequently, the resonance moves toward that which is unclarified and deliberately equivocal.

Within this mythical reduction, the characters no longer exist in an actual movement from the depths to the heights, identifying themselves as celebrants in a myth or numinous ritual; rather they construct an image of nature, a safe and unthreatening—and artificial—world which translates the substance of life into an ordered, protective, safe environment which only gives the illusion of the primitive and the wild.

In the control of plausibility which is working upon the complexity and density of Ibsen's drama of consciousness in *The Wild Duck*, the image of the mythical and the formal which is abstracted in clearer metaphors in plays such as *Brand* and *Emperor and Galilean* is displaced into the strange and yet realistic image of the garret. The garret is an image of form and timelessness, a place of innocence, a created environment which is the manifestation of the will—and yet the substance of that image is phenomenal experience itself. That phenomenal substance is the content of the illusion used by Old Ekdal, Hjalmar, and Hedvig. The garret provides the illusion of phenomenal experience without the threat—except, of course, the recurrent recognition in Ibsen that the choice of the mythical is the acceptance of death.

The sacrifice of Hedvig is the result of her glimpse of the sky and the sea. Hedvig's death is not the consequence of reality intruding upon her own imagination so much as it is the consequence of the reality of the past intruding upon the illusion of a normal family housed in the Ekdal residence. In a sense, the death is caused by the clarification of the truth of Hjalmar's situation; that revelation demonstrates to him that his whole life is a kind of illusion. Gregers's act of clarification destroys, at least temporarily, Hjalmar's illusory life. The sacrifice of Hedvig is the result of Hjalmar's knowledge of the biological fact of her identity—that Old Werle is the source of her being as he is the source of all that exists in Hjalmar's world.

The conflict in *The Wild Duck* seems to take an atypical form in comparison with Ibsen's other major plays in that there is not the usual triad of a protagonist whose inner struggles are projected in his relationship with two women, each demanding a course antithetical to the other. The same kind of struggle exists here but the tension is distributed in a different arrangement of characters. Initially, one is struck by the absence of a normal family unit; both Hjalmar and Gregers have been dominated by women. Hjalmar has been raised by two aunts; and, from the perspective of psychological reality, he is the victim of this experience. Gregers is the child of a strained and unhappy union between his aggressively exploitative father and a woman whom that union drove into insanity. He himself suffers her jaded vision—her sense of the ideal and, even more critically, her cynical and despairing attitude. The images of Gregers's demented mother and Hjalmar's aunts—women who embodied the claim of the ideal—provide the recurrent image of an ascetic denial of sexuality in opposition to the sensually robust female. In a sense, these unseen and dead figures from the past form the denying female to counter the presence of the warm and vital Gina.

Neither Hjalmar nor Gregers is a successful man. Both are failures in terms of sexual identity. Gregers has inherited both the ugliness and the despair of his mother; and although he exerts a strong influence on the action of the drama, the resolution of that action is not the consequence of his will. Hjalmar is unable to earn a living to support his own family and lives in ignorance of the fact that he is not the breadwinner. Hjalmar's single claim to a strong male identity, his fathering of Hedvig, is removed from him. Like Old Werle, the single strong male of Ibsen's play, he is selfish and exploitative; but, unlike Werle, he is neither strong, nor capable, nor wise.

The deterioration of the hero in *The Wild Duck* results in the play being an ironic structure, one in which the vision is despairing and pessimistic. Instead of the strong conflict between vocation and "the joy of life," usually projected in the pleasures and responsibilities of family or in the image of a sexually attractive woman, we have the explicitly illusory escape of Hjalmar's invention. Vocation is a metaphor for the hero's attempt to come to terms with the world outside of his own consciousness and an attempt to determine some kind of order in experience. In each version of Ibsen's drama that attempt is a futile act; but it is a conscious, deliberate effort of the will, a sincere and assertive attempt. In Hjalmar's case that vocation is only a rationalization. The time devoted to his invention is in actuality a time spent sleeping, and the pages of his technical books remain uncut. Also, the idea of the invention comes to him externally. It is the "life-lie," the sustaining illusion of purpose therapeutically administered by Dr. Relling; it is analogous to Molvik's concept of his demonic state which is a rationalization of his alcoholism.

Of course, in the division of the function of protagonist in *The Wild Duck*, Gregers Werle also has a vocation: the claim of the ideal. This vocation is futile and destructive; it confronts the victims with the truth of their victimization and provides them with no sustaining notions of order to render that truth acceptable or even bearable. Gregers is a stranger who intrudes into the family, revealing the past and latent hostilities of the present, but unlike the female version of this Ibsen catalyst, Gregers is strangely unerotic. He is, however, somewhat mysterious. He suggests at several points in the play that he is not to live much longer. The last line of the play in which he states that he is to suffer the destiny of being thirteenth at table is a reference to that fate as well. Certainly *The Wild Duck* is concerned with regressive movements which Ibsen poses as movements toward a death in life, and Gregers's mysterious future is part of that concern.

While the basic antithesis of illusion and truth in *The Wild Duck* seems relatively obvious, this version of Ibsen's drama of the determining will has a complex and difficult structure. Certainly Relling and Gregers define the conflict. Relling defends the adaptation to experience made in the development of a sustaining illusion.

RELLING.   I am supposed to be a sort of doctor, it's a shame to say. And so I must help those poor sufferers with whom I share a house.

GREGERS.   Is that so! Hjalmar Ekdal is sick also? . . . and what treatment are you giving Hjalmar?

RELLING.   My usual one. I am cultivating the "life-lie" in him.

GREGERS.   Life-lie? I didn't hear correctly.

RELLING.   Yes, I said "life-lie." For the "life-lie" is the stimulating principle, you see.

Relling goes on to describe how he has helped Molvik by giving him the illusion that he is demonic; and then he discusses Old Ekdal's accommodation, an adaptation which the old man arrived at by himself:

What do you think of him, the old bear-hunter going into that dark garret and hunting rabbits? There isn't a happier rifleman in the world than he, that old man, when he goes playing about among all that rubbish. The four or five withered Christmas trees which he has saved, they are the same to him as the whole, spacious fresh Hoidal Forest; the cock and all the hens, they are big game birds in the tops of the pine trees, and the rabbits which jump around on the floor of the garret, they are bears which he wrestles with, the strong old outdoorsman!

Relling then describes the idealism of Gregers Werle as another illusion: "Don't use that foreign word: ideals. We have, you know, that good Norwegian word: lies."

Relling has often been described as Ibsen's voice in *The Wild Duck*, and yet the antithesis seems not to be

simple enough to allow that direct association. The kind
of illusory retreat used by Hjalmar at Relling's instiga-
tion is, certainly, destructive. The Ekdals' escape to "the
bottom of the sea" after suffering injury in the hostile
world contributes to the destructive consequence of
Hedvig's death in action with Gregers's catalyst. The demand of sacrifice is as much Hjalmar's demand to
Hedvig as it is Gregers's. Hjalmar feels that Hedvig will
be tempted to leave his home and go to her natural father
since he can offer her wealth and comfort:

> If the others came, they with their hands overflowing,
> and called to the child: leave him; with us you have
> life waiting for you— . . . If then I asked her:
> Hedvig, you are willing to give up that life for me?
> (*laughs derisively*)—No, thank you! You would hear
> soon enough what answer I should get. (A *pistol shot
> is heard from the garret.*)

In one sense Hedvig renounces life itself for her father
in response to his demand for proof of her love. He confesses to Gregers that he has no faith in the reality of her
love, and her suicide is related to the suicide of Rebekka
in *Rosmersholm*, an act which answers Johannes's demand for absolute proof of the integrity of her love.
Johannes works to clarify the reality of Rebekka's love
and also to eliminate the possibility that the sexuality of
their relationship will continue to threaten him. In *The
Wild Duck*, in which the implicit eroticism is more oblique, the latent demand for Hedvig's death is not present because she herself, as a character within the play,
threatens Hjalmar in a direct sensual sense. However, her
death—the death of the child becoming a woman—is
the major aspect of a series of movements away from
sexuality in the play. It is the ultimate image of regression, the clearest retreat to "the bottom of the sea." As
well, this death is the paradoxical application of the
claim of the ideal; and the futility of that action comes in
the prediction which Relling makes of Hjalmar's use of
the event:

We shall talk of this again when the first grass has withered on her grave. Then you will be able to hear him regurgitate about "the child torn too soon from her father's heart." Then you will see him immerse himself in sentimentality and in self-admiration and self-pity. You watch!

This strong prediction devalues the sacrifice as an event which clarifies reality for Hjalmar in Relling's suggestion that his grief will become merely another aspect of his illusory self-justification, working with his fictitious invention as a strategy to give himself an image of worth.

However, the process of adaptation or accommodation which in part could be considered the real *act* of Ibsen's play is also made equivocal in that Werle's "claim of the ideal" is not merely an approach to reality but is, for Gregers himself, a form of adaptation or accommodation. Ibsen reveals, through Relling, that Gregers uses Hjalmar in substitution for his own identity. He describes Hjalmar and Gregers's relationship to him:

> Ekdal's bad fortune is that within his own circle he has always been held up as a shining light . . . when our beloved, sweet Hjalmar became a student, he was immediately considered to be the great light of the future among his companions. He was certainly handsome, the idler—red and white—the sort which young girls become infatuated with; he with his easily moved temperament and compelling voice, and his pretty ability to declaim the poetry of others and the thoughts of others. . . . for that is the inner nature of this idol which you grovel before.

Relling continues, telling Gregers that he, too, is diseased:

> First there is that troublesome, self-righteous, fevered frenzy, and then what is worse, you are always in an incoherent delirium of worship; you must always have something to admire beyond yourself.

Gregers responds: "Yes, I must certainly seek that respect outside of myself." Gregers's use of Hjalmar is motivated by his own need. In the clarification of the relationship of Gregers and Hjalmar, we see that what has addressed itself as pure altruism, "the claim of the ideal," has had an exploitative function: Gregers is using Hjalmar in his own adaptation to the world of reality. Hjalmar's identity is Gregers's illusion. Hjalmar's restoration is the specific implementation of Gregers's vocation.

Certainly one of the interests of this play is the attenuation and distribution of the major images of the Ibsen canon: the diminishing use of the metaphor of vocation, the reduction of the hero's notion of the power of his own will, the distribution of the typical tensions working upon the hero from the usual pair of women to the series of conflicts between illusion and reality or adaptation and confrontation. There remains, however distorted and disguised, the tension between the ascetic and the erotic. The strong image of guilt which in *Brand* voices itself in the image of Gerd is only barely visible in *The Wild Duck* in the image of Gregers's mother—the woman who shares with Beate in *Rosmersholm* the maddening torment of her husband's infidelity. As well, the brief references to Hjalmar's past and his virtuous and doting aunts relate these dead women and the demands which they put upon their nephew to the usual structure of an erotic and an ascetic woman battling for the life of the hero. But the battle has been waged and won in *The Wild Duck* before the play begins. There is no Rita, no Hilde, no Rebekka, nor even Agnes in this play. Gina hardly qualifies. In this work the presence of sexuality is submerged, disguised, and only barely reaches the surface in the awakening sexuality of Hedvig.

Each illusion in *The Wild Duck*, each adaptation, is a form of the denial of the erotic. Gregers's conflict with his father is primarily concerned with an attack upon his father's exploitative sexuality, and Gregers's maintenance of his mother's attitude is in itself a denial of his own sexuality. Hjalmar's adaptation to social injury is a denial of his own masculinity in that he surrenders his will even in these matters to Old Werle who not only provides for the family but also fathers his child. While we have no sense of sexual estrangement between Hjalmar and Gina as we do in *Rosmersholm*, *The Master Builder*, and *Little Eyolf*, the marriage itself is barren and Hjalmar has never assumed the leadership of the family or even the fulfillment of the tasks of his prosaic vocation.

Here the relationship of Hjalmar and Hedvig is crucial. In the first place, Hedvig represents an extension of Hjalmar's identity, a proof of his manliness which proves to be an illusion. She initially seems to be some sort of promise for him, some image of the future; however, that promise is ambiguous, because her blindness clarifies his own injury. Hedvig's approaching blindness is part of the sorrow Hjalmar's life encompasses. An understanding of the relationship between light and darkness, blindness and the confrontation with reality is difficult and yet crucial to an understanding of *The Wild Duck*. The one character who seems to see reality as it is, who bears witness to the hostility of nature and uses its energies with facility is, of course, Grosserer Werle. And yet Werle himself is going blind. He is being restricted, contained, detached from reality and is moving from the city to the woods at Hoidal with all the metaphorical implications which that action holds.

In these terms, the metaphor of photography is very important. Here surely is the sense of a blatant, uncompromising reflection of external reality which does not respond to its complexities and latent content. Also, Hjalmar himself does not practice photography but does, upon occasion, retouch. Ibsen removes him from the kind of confrontation with reality which the craft of photography would imply, and it is important that his action in withdrawing from responsibility in the studio leads Hedvig into the job of retouching. Hedvig herself is interested in art; she is inspired by the engraving found in the garret (but those engravings are associated with death); her vocation, however, is closed off by the prediction of blindness and then suddenly by death. From the time we hear of it her desire to become an artist is futile and offers no promise in itself.

Hedvig's desire to be an engraver suggests an extension of Hjalmar's desire to discover some method of transporting photography from a craft into an art; and yet her desire to work as an artist within the bounds of her family also recalls Hjalmar's fearful retreat into the security of his situation:

GREGERS.   Tell me, now, when you are sitting in there and looking at pictures, don't you ever wish to get out and see the great real world for yourself?

HEDVIG.   No, not at all. I want to stay here at home always and help father and mother.

GREGERS.   To retouch photographs?

HEDVIG.   No, not that alone. Most of all I should like to learn to engrave pictures like those in the English books.

Yet we know that this hope will never come true because of her blindness. This injury comes from her true relationship to Werle, and it is this injury which clarifies that relationship in Hjalmar's imagination. The blindness injures both in two directions. It is important to realize that the image of promise which Hedvig would offer to Hjalmar is presented as being damaged from the beginning of the action of the play. The death of Hedvig, for Hjalmar, is a completion of the destruction of the promise. In one sense, this *Kindermord* is the destruction of the illusion which sustains Hjalmar. And yet it is much more than that.

The suicide of Hedvig is the completion of Hjalmar's act of denying her. It is the consequence of his demand for sacrifice to prove her love of him; and it is, beyond the relationship with Hjalmar and in the context of the tensions which bind the whole work together, the critical denial of sexuality. In Hjalmar's case this denial (the killing of Hedvig) is the ultimate rejection of sensuality or the erotic which is the form of his withdrawal from reality into illusion. In Hedvig's case it is important to consider the process of her identification with the wild duck. For her the act is both a proof and an escape. It is a desperate clarification of the "truth" of her identity as Hjalmar's child. She is, in essence, giving herself to him as child and at the same moment, taking herself away. Her suicide is the complete acceptance of the validity of the metaphorical "bottom of the sea" which, for Hedvig, is the same psychological condition as the woods are for Hjalmar and Old Ekdal. Hedvig accepts the regressive movement into the fictive world of illusion in ultimate terms; in her imagination she becomes the wild duck which must be sacrificed, and this action of identification with the fictive is a total rejection of the real world to the point of death.

It is important to recognize that in Ibsen's plays sacrifice is not redemptive. Ibsen deliberately undercuts the positive qualities of the act which would be contained in its archetypal associations with Relling's description of Hjalmar's probable use of the event. Hedvig will become the vessel for Hjalmar's illusory life. She could not, in reality, have remained his child; the presence of the real Hedvig would have been a constant reminder of the reality of her identity. However, in death she is transformed from a clarification of the hostility of reality into the unchanging innocence and goodness of the illusion of Hedvig as Hjalmar's child. In death, she can remain an image, unsullied; child, not woman; the proof of his fatherhood, not the evidence of his failure.

Hedvig's association of the garret and the sea provides part of the strangeness of this play, and yet an understanding of Ibsen's use of this metaphor reveals the meaning of its verbal structure despite the obvious disguises present in this play. The closed scene of *The Wild Duck*, the restricted environment of the surrogate woods, for example, and the contained atmosphere of the Ekdal home, limit the possibility of the presence of the real sea which informs many of the other plays. Here the sea as metaphor is present only in the little story of the wild duck and in the few evocations of it. Twice Hjalmar sees his father as "shipwrecked," and the presence of the mysterious captain, the Flying Dutchman, with his associations of sacrifice and death at sea pervade the garret and inform our response to this place. And, of course, in Hedvig's imagination the garret is "the bottom of the sea." In a perceptive discussion of the image patterns in Ibsen's play, Brian Johnston discusses the use of the metaphor of the sea in *The Wild Duck*:

> Metaphors of freedom are associated with the sea, and with sailors and sea-creatures, and those of rebellion, with fire. The fascination in watching or reading Ibsen is in seeing the way in which these huge poetic metaphors discipline themselves under the requirements of modern realism. . . . When . . . Hedvig records her horror at *her* Flying Dutchman's engraving of Death, an Hour-Glass, and a Girl, she is experiencing a thrill of premonition, for a destiny has been laid upon her as upon Senta. With this in mind we must certainly see Hedvig's suicide as a more positive action than most accounts allow. In the attic, in the depths of the sea, the surviving yet unplaced spirit of romantic idealism and aspiration to ultimate freedom still faintly lurks, waiting for one human being capable of the supreme idealistic gesture of self-sacrifice.[2]

As Johnston points out, a sense of freedom, escape, a concept of unrestricted spirit is certainly one aspect of Ibsen's use of the image of the sea. However, that aspect of the image is only its *temptation*, its *lure*. The illusion of freedom is what the tempting sea offers its victims. In Ibsen's drama, the sea tempts and then consumes; those who surrender to the lure of freedom may release themselves from the binding restrictive snares of prosaic responsibility and ethical demand, but the acceptance of this freedom and the denial of life it assumes is, irredeemably, the acceptance of death. Ibsen's use of the sea is, in many ways, analogous to his use of the image of the heights (and recall that Hedvig imagines that she has seen the sea from the heights). For example, as we shall see later, Solness's climb to the top of the tower, away from the earth and its binding demands, is as suicidal as is Hedvig's acceptance of the metaphor of sacrifice at "the bottom of the sea." Freedom is disguised in this sense; and to deny the association with death which is implict in Ibsen's metaphor of the sea is to ignore the larger meaning in his metaphoric structures. In *The Wild Duck* the sea is a dream or illusion of freedom, not, as Johnston says, freedom itself. Its symbolism is dream imagery and it shares with the woods the function of being an escape from the pain and injury and deprivation and futility and loneliness of reality. But the retreat into the sea and into the woods is a regressive movement; it is a withdrawal from real experience. It does have, as does Hilde's and Solness's creation of castles in the air, an energy or vitality which gives it a sense of beauty and a value within the play; but that beauty and value are fictive and ultimately destructive. Ibsen underlines this futility in his clear implication that Hedvig's suicide is futile, meaningless in terms of Hjalmar's real vision of reality. It is not, ultimately, an assertion against the hostility of nature. It is rather another form of adaptation or accommodation, and it will become part of Hjalmar's acceptance or adaptation.

The Wild Duck differs greatly, both in structure and technique from the preceding plays, but it is typical in its use of the past intruding upon the present. The action of clarification is again primary. But this play, perhaps even more clearly than *Ghosts*, demonstrates that the past as menace in Ibsen is less a projection of past deeds affecting present conditions as it is a clarification of what is latent in the present. The movement of *The Wild Duck* is not toward a sense of the inevitability of the past avenging itself, as the woods claim their revenge, but rather is a movement toward the realization of the structure of the present. The fear of an unsuppressed confrontation with reality is acute in *The Wild Duck*. The complex of built illusions is proof of the threaten-

ing nature of that confrontation. The primary fact of
the avoided reality is Old Werle's fathering of Hedvig—
the fact that this creature, protected and kept childlike,
is, in truth, the product of a sexual relationship between
Old Werle and Gina. In one sense, Grosserer Werle
represents either the hostility of nature itself or some one
who is able to use the energies of nature in the assertion
of his own desire. In Gregers's case the desire he experiences to be the instrumentality of a true marriage
based upon a mutual recognition of truth seems to be a
wish to redeem his father's nature, to expiate his father's
sin and transform the reality of the situation into an
idealized dream of marriage. In any case, the movement
he makes toward the implementation of that desire is,
from one perspective at least, the product of his fear that
the aggressive sexuality of his father is the only reality.

It is certainly obvious that Ibsen is working within the
form of irony which Northrop Frye defines. His scene is
clearly the fallen world in which there is no possibility of
redemption. All of his characters are injured, diseased,
incapable, or inadequate. Through the directing metaphor of the wild duck, Gregers associates himself with
the "incredibly clever dog" which follows the duck down
into the depths of the sea and retrieves it from the tangles
of sea grass in which it is suicidally entangled in what
seems to be an instinctive movement. The naturalness
of the suicidal dive is crucial to this imitation of the
fallen world. The dog, of course, returns the bird to a
life which offers an adaptation to a reduced, contained,
attenuated life or—if the freedom of the sky and sea is
glimpsed again—certain death. In Gregers's terms, he is
retrieving Hjalmar from the poisonous depths into the
light; and he expects that this movement from ignorance
and adaptation will be one of transfiguration. He does
not see that the dog has injured the duck and that this
escape from death is not redemptive. Ibsen poses the
analogy between adaptation and death as a kind of equation; and the new home of the duck becomes the "bottom of the sea," the place of her death in life. Gregers

expects the Ekdal home, once exposed to truth, to become filled with transforming light:

> I had expected, so certainly, that when I came through the door that I would be struck with a light of transfiguration shining upon me from both husband and wife. And now I see nothing other than dullness, oppressiveness, and sadness.

Redemption or transfiguration in the world of *The Wild Duck* is only possible within illusion, and the play closes upon that final illusion—the image of the dead Hedvig, transformed in her father's imagination into the illusion of innocence and his own pure suffering. Gregers's realization that this use of the sacrifice is probable moves him into despair and a devaluation of life itself. Within this realistic portrayal of ordinary people, Ibsen has once more imitated a complex movement of consciousness in which some illusory or mythical concept of reality fails, destroying the ground on which identity is based. And in the resolution of this play, there is the clear but difficult act of reconstituting the myth in some attenuated form. In this case, the final movement toward myth is not the clear movement of the hero toward death. Here the death of the child stabilizes the myth in time, and the death of the hero is reduced to Hjalmar's impotence and failure and Gregers's vague comments which suggest that he himself might end his life if Relling's vision is true.

5

Rosmersholm

Rosmersholm, which follows *The Wild Duck* immediately, was completed and published in 1886. Both plays
reveal the essential drama of consciousness by carefully
penetrating a dense realistic surface, exposing the nature
of those tensions which hold that surface together. However, while each play is written within a realistic form,
they are very different. In *The Wild Duck* the basic
tension between the mythical and the phenomenal is
distributed among several figures who enact the central
drama. A pathetic group of injured people form a collective community in this play, and through the incon-
clusive resolution, Ibsen projects the possibility that
they will continue together, injured more deeply, but
supporting their mutual illusions. In *The Wild Duck*
Ibsen almost offers a definition of a benevolent society
as the cohesive structure formed to protect the individual's mythical strategy.

Rosmersholm also concerns injured and weakened
people. Even the vitality of Rebekka West, which manifests itself destructively, is an aspect of the past. Rebekka is the tempting female, but unlike her earlier
counterparts, she is a fully developed character. The
wholeness of her characterization, which contains the
basic conflict itself, extends the meaning of Rosmer's
experience into the most complete statement which Ibsen was yet to make concerning the mythological process
in human consciousness. The complex image of Rebekka

focuses the tension in Rosmer's imagination between the mythical and the phenomenal and reveals its paradox to him. All of the metaphoric lines meet in Rebekka.

In *The Wild Duck*, one of the images of form and perhaps the central metaphor of that very complex play is the image of the garret. This strange place is the dramatic embodiment of a process of consciousness which attempts to contain or encompass phenomenal experience by creating an illusion of it. This illusion seems harmless; however, the movement into the apparent sanctaury is, in truth, a suicide. The real forest and the real sea do avenge themselves in the Ekdal's experience —they are the metaphors of phenomenal experience, and they destroy the image of selfhood. The sanctuary from that experience, the garret, is equally destructive and tempts Hedvig into suicide. The garret is a difficult image, but it is clearly one of Ibsen's transforming metaphors which seem to provide a sense of form and then dissolve into formlessness. In this sense, the garret is related to the metaphor of the Ice Church. The extreme movement into the state of consciousnes which these images suggest accomplishes its opposite: the movement into safety is a confrontation with those energies which that sanctuary attempts to contain.

In the frozen form of the Ice Church and the contained enclosure of the garret, Ibsen projects a concept of the attempt to hold the processes of phenomenal experience within some restrictive form. The Ice Church is the static symbol of will achieved in Brand's imagination, and the garret encloses the forest and the sea; but neither metaphor of form can contain these energies and bursts open, revealing its inadequacy as form. *Rosmersholm* reveals new aspects of this basic drama. Hedvig and the garret in *The Wild Duck*, and the whole paradigm of illusions and "life-lies" are the embodiments of the mythical strategy of consciousness. In *Rosmersholm* Rebekka West fills that function, but her role is inclusively ambiguous. She is the focal point of antithetical desires in Rosmer's imagination—the dream of an ascetic, innocent, timeless sense of being and the dream of sexual pleasure without guilt. Rebekka is the image of form which is transformed into its opposite in the imagination of the hero.

In the early moments of the play Rosmer seems divided between a clearly defined antithesis—the restrictive and oppressive past of the Rosmer tradition, which includes an aggressive ethic, and the promise of a new freedom with Rebekka which includes a life based upon a natural morality. As the play progresses, the ambiguity of that basic antithesis becomes increasingly clear; and the primary action of *Rosmersholm* is the clarification of that ambiguity in consciousness. In the first scene of the play the images which suggest restriction and oppression relate to the past, and images of light, growth, and pleasure describe the quality of the present. The scene is Rosmersholm, a country estate which is the home of Johannes Rosmer, the area's most important social figure. His wife, Beate, died within the past year, and her companion, Rebekka West, remains in the household to care for Rosmer and to manage the home. She is a lovely, vital young woman who seems to have brought a sense of light and warmth into the house which had been darkened by a sense of gloom and depression with the physical illness and mental disturbance of Beate Rosmer. Kroll, Beate's brother makes the following observation when he calls upon them for the first time after his sister's death:

KROLL. . . . Why, how cozy and attractive you have made the old living room. Flowers all around.

REBEKKA. Rosmer very much likes to have fresh, living flowers around him.

KROLL. And you, too, I imagine.

REBEKKA. Yes. I seem to be quieted by their loveliness. Before we had to deprive ourselves of that pleasure.

KROLL (*nodding sadly*). Poor Beate couldn't endure their odor.

REBEKKA. Nor their color, either. She became wildly
    confused—

Ibsen suggests that Rebekka's energy and youth will
transform the nature of Rosmersholm itself as Johannes
moves closer to her. Rosmersholm is a dense image in
this play which discloses the powerful demand that the
past and all it claims is able to make upon those who live
in the present. Rosmersholm is both a physical location,
the center of the province and the core of its tradition,
and an ethical attitude. Its perspective is familial;
Rosmer is bound to a concept of family structure which
determines his ethical decisions, his professional career
(the Rosmers move in alternating generations between
the army and the clergy), his political attitude, and his
style of life. The Rosmer "view of life" is bound to an
ascetic Christian morality which denies the value of
sensual pleasure. This family-centered tradition asserts
itself in the present. The visual image of the walls cov-
ered with "old and more recent portraits of clergymen,
officers, and government officials in uniform" maintains
our awareness of that assertion. Kroll defines the traditional demand which the Rosmersholm ethic makes
upon Johannes:

> Rosmers of Rosmersholm, priests and army officers.
> Highly respected government officials. Proper gentle-
> men—all of them. A family which has held its place
> as first in this district for two hundred years. . . . You
> owe it to yourself and your family tradition to join in
> defending all of the proven values of our community.

His definition of the Rosmer tradition is a rhetorical
scheme to persuade Rosmer to support his cause, his
conservative defense of his own authority within society,
his school, and his family.

The association of Rosmersholm, the place and the
spiritual condition, with the past is clear. That sense of
past, however, is bound together with the corresponding
concept of death. The image of the white horses suggests

the dead exerting some claim upon the living. The characters in the play see that claim as an external demand, but Ibsen clarifies that the image of the white horses is a metaphor for acute internal demands. Ibsen's use of this metaphor illustrates his dramatic strategy of gradually exposing the content of his major dramatic image. Initially the white horses seem to be a simple image of the past, but that simplicity is qualified and complicated throughout the play. The association of the image and Rosmersholm itself suggests that the Rosmer tradition is related to the sense of death; the Rosmer dead return to claim those who still live. The metaphor of the white horses is also used as an image of onrushing energy; this sense relates Beate to this vision even more clearly. Her "frenzied passion" is an image of energy which is analogous to the sense of irrational power in the coursing of the white horses. As we explore the opposition of energy and calm contained in the figure of Rebekka West, the use of the image of the white horse as a metaphor of sexual energy will be clearer. At this point, however, it is necesary to see that Rosmer's conception of Beate, who is the specific character from the past abstracted into an image of the dead who claim the living, is apparently untroubled and calm. Ibsen subtly suggests that Rosmer either pretends or mistakenly believes that Beate's memory neither causes him to suffer nor is the source of any guilt. He tells Kroll:

> There is nothing painful for me in the thought of Beate. We speak of her every day. She seems to be living here still, somehow, we feel. . . . We both were so deeply fond of her. Both Rebek—both Miss West and I know that we did everything in our power for her in her suffering. We have nothing to reproach ourselves for. So I feel that there is something mild and gentle in thinking about Beate.

Rosmer's sense of Beate's presence is ambiguous; her demanding presence will manifest itself in his consciousness as an embodiment of his guilt later in the play.

Here his description of his peaceful memory of Beate conflicts with the information revealed earlier by Rebekka who despairs that he always avoids the footbridge over the millrace where Beate's suicide took place. Rebekka's observation is the motive for the introduction of the telling image of the white horses and the declaration that the dead cling to the living at Rosmersholm. Rosmer's sense of tranquility is clearly a surface calm.

The primary action in *Rosmersholm* is a movement from an illusory tranquility which is in reality an uneasy and chaotic period of turmoil in which the latent eroticism of Rebekka's and Rosmer's relationship is avoided, to a confrontation of the sexual base of their union, and then into the calm stasis of death in an act which is seen in images of rushing energy. This movement is revealed in two basic transformations in Rosmer's imagination: the transition in his conception of both Beate and Rebekka. Rosmer's change is the result of the disclosure of his relationship with Rebekka. The disclosure is forced by Kroll's intrusion into their private world. Their world is protected by secretiveness, and the surface of their companionship which pretends to be nonerotic is destroyed by the public condemnation of it as sexual.

In Rosmer's imagination, Beate had been protected, cared for, and shielded from the truth of his apostasy. He thinks that she was able to maintain an image of him as the Johannes Rosmer who held the faith and ethical attitude of his fathers. His relationship with Rebekka is protected by the maintenance of that illusion, and it is destroyed by the disclosure of its reality. Part of that disclosure comes from Beate herself through her letter to Mortensgaard. When Johannes learns from Mortensgaard that Beate was not protected from that crucial knowledge, his sense of Beate as a demanding energy which voices his guilt becomes clearer. Beate is also directly associated with sexuality in Rosmer's imagination; he speaks to Kroll: "I have told you about her wild, frenzied passion—which she demanded I return. Oh, how she filled me with horror!" Rosmer is the product

of Rosmersholm's ascetic ethic, and the overt sexuality of
Beate is repellent to him. He denies her in this sense, and
she is herself the victim of Rosmersholm. Beate is childless, and it is her inability to bear children which is said
to be the cause of her hysteria. The images of *child* and
childlessness are crucial to an understanding of *Rosmersholm*, and yet the function of this metaphoric antithesis
is oblique and frequently obscure. Certainly this motive
is related to the recurrent image of infanticide, *Kindermord*, and childlessness throughout Ibsen. Recall, for
example, Brand's renunciation of Alf and his conception
of Alf's death as an expiation of Brand's mother's sin.
Brand's denial of his son is an attempt to halt the relentless transmission of guilt from one generation to the
next. Rosmer sees the oppressive ethic of Rosmersholm
in that same unyielding course of inheritance—a vision of
guilt passing from generation to generation. That guilt
is a tangible reality in Rosmer's imagination, and eventually the need of its expiation makes its demands on
him. The image of *child* in Ibsen also is the focal point
of a dream of innocence. The relationship between
childhood and innocence is voiced in memories of youth,
as in Julian's vision of his childhood in the light and air
of Makellon, and in two specific characters—Alf and
Hedvig. Childhood is innocent because it is free of the
destructive processes of sexuality.

Hedvig stands at the point of transition between child
and woman, and she is also identified with Hjalmar as
the proof of his manliness. In the reality of the world in
The Wild Duck she cannot remain such an image. She
is actually the injured child of Werle's sexual use of
Gina, and she can only maintain her identity as
Hjalmar's child in illusion. Hjalmar needs Hedvig as the
proof of his own identity, and she sacrifices herself to
maintain that illusion. The sacrificed child is a recurrent
figure in Ibsen, and each sacrifice reveals an aspect of the
consciousness of the hero. Frequently the death of the
child works to clarify a psychic event in the consciousness
of the hero; usually that movement includes the dis-

integration of some illusion of innocence. Surely it is significant that Beate is barren, that the relationship of Rosmer and Beate is *childless*. Rebekka declares that it is better for Rosmer that he had no children, since he is not a man to be burdened with the sound of children crying. In response Madam Helspeth gives a strange description of children born at Rosmersholm:

> . . . small children do not cry at Rosmersholm . . . on this estate small children have not been in the habit of crying for as long as people can remember. . . . it runs in the family. And there is another strange thing. When they grow up, they never laugh.

Rosmersholm, in some way, injures its children. Rosmer has suffered that injury. He is unable to laugh despite the fact that he feels he has a "great aptitude for happiness." The childlessness of Rosmersholm works to clarify the strength of the guilt which is the primary quality of that emotional condition which the whole Rosmersholm family paradigm embodies. Within that condition of guilt, no manifestation of innocence can exist, and there is only the perverted displacement of the innocence of childhood in Rosmer's conception of his union with Rebekka as "childlike." Rosmer confesses to Rebekka: "When we were together, I felt joyous, calm, desireless happiness. When we think about it truthfully, Rebekka, our life together began as a sweet, secret, *child-love*." In his imagination their relationship is childlike and innocent; it is calm and not subject to the energies of sexuality. As such, it is the antithesis of the childlessness of Beate which is related to guilt. Rosmer's sense of his child-love with Rebekka is an illusion in which he can dream of a timeless relationship, free of the processes and guilt of sexuality.

It is also revealing that Rosmer describes his relationship with Rebekka as a "*secret* child-love." Both Rosmer and Rebekka have worked to keep their relationship hidden. The public disclosure of that strange companionship destroys it. In a sense the exposure is the revelation of a lie; their life together is not overtly licentious. And yet the truth of that disclosure, the implicit sexuality of their relationship, is clarified both to the public and to Rosmer himself. His fear of that ultimate disclosure is implicit in this speech:

> I thought that sooner or later our beautiful, pure, companionship would be soiled and made the object of suspicion. . . . Oh, yes, I had good reason for concealing our alliance so jealously. It was a dangerous secret.

The real danger of that secret, of course, is that the actual content of their companionship was hidden from Rosmer himself. His greatest fear is guilt, and underneath his illusion of the "beautiful, pure companionship" is the aggressive reality of his own sexuality. The disclosure of that reality transforms the image of Rebekka West in his consciousness.

The center of Rebekka's vitality is her passion for Rosmer. Initially Rebekka's energy is seen as natural, regenerative, full of light in antithesis to the images directed to Beate who is seen in terms of darkness, oppression, morbidity. However, Ibsen presents both Beate and Rebekka surrendering to the ethic of Rosmersholm, and both sacrifice themselves for Rosmer. Rebekka acts out the same suicide as Beate, and both see themselves destroyed by the demands which Rosmer puts upon them—Beate implicitly and Rebekka explicitly. Both women threaten Rosmer's innocence and are willing to kill themselves rather than to continue to cause him pain. Beate, of course, dies in the delusion that she is preparing the way for the birth of the child of Rebekka and Rosmer. That child does not exist and could not exist within the present condition of Rosmersholm.

Both Rebekka and Beate are directed by lust, and they are seen as images of a consuming energy. Curiously that energy is seen as a force which exists only in the past. Both of them have suffered the restraining ethic of Rosmersholm. In Beate's case, that restraining ethic is transferred to her and she becomes its agent. The imagined presence of the dead Beate is a voice from the past, and her presence takes the form of the image of the white horses, those supernatural creatures which signal the dead claiming the living at Rosmersholm. As Rebekka's innocence dissolves in Rosmer's imagination, he feels the increasingly strong presence of Beate. He feels his wife clinging to him, and he cries out to Rebekka: "I will not go through life with a corpse on my back! Help me to cast it off, Rebekka!" Beate, of course, has no more reality to Rosmer than that which is formed by his own consciousness. In that sense, Rebekka is truthful in her declaration that the living cling to their dead at Rosmersholm. The increasing vitality of Beate's imagined presence is one of the means by which the past intrudes upon the present in *Rosmersholm*. Beate, with the implication of sanctity and blessing, is the specific past in *Rosmersholm*, qualifying the present of the damned.

The developing presence of Beate which parallels the disintegrating innocence of Rebekka is clarified as Ibsen characterizes Rebekka as the victim of her own uncontrollable sexual energy. Both the image of the rushing white horses and the image of the rushing water of the millrace are related to the sense of passion or energy which overtakes the will. This association is even clearer in Rebekka's description of the irrationality which compelled her to delude Beate:

> It was a wild uncontrollable desire. . . . It came over me like a storm at sea. It was like one of the storms which we can have in the North in the wintertime. It takes you, and carries you along with it—as far as it goes. It is impossible to resist it.

Ibsen's metaphor of the sea voices itself indirectly in *Rosmersholm*, but it is clear in Rebekka's description of her violent lust. The millrace becomes a displaced image of the sea as a body of rushing water which lures Beate and Rebekka and Rosmer to it. Rosmer sees

Beate's death in the millrace as the final scene of her passion. In this sense, the sexual energy of each of these figures drives them to the sea or, at least, the attenuated image of the sea.

Rebekka is related to the sea in another strange sense as well. Rebekka is undeniably a temptress. Obviously, she once attracted Kroll himself and used him to introduce herself into the Rosmer household. Her ability to attract men is sounded in Brendel's "alluring mermaid," and when she faces the alternatives of death and a damaged life with Rosmer, she says: "After today I would only be a sea-troll, hanging onto and restraining the ship on which you should sail forward." Rebekka and Beate are both related to the white horses which lure the living Rosmer to death; and as Rebekka enacts Beate's suicide, she clothes herself in the white shawl which she has been making throughout the play. Mrs. Helspeth sees that white figure as the white horses come to claim their dead.

The analogy between Rebekka and Beate who are initially defined as extremes of a complex antithesis derives from the fact that the insistent dialectic in *Rosmersholm* is a struggle which takes place in the consciousness of Rosmer himself. The figure of Rebekka West does have a density and psychological validity which gives her a sense of being almost as compelling as Rosmer's own, but she exists primarily to provide an object for Rosmer's own action. She is the transforming object toward which his energy moves. Rebekka's eroticism is disclosed to him, and this revelation of the sexual ground of their relationship makes it impossible for him to continue within the illusion of their tranquil, innocent relationship. Her reality within his consciousness changes, and he moves from latent unexpressed desire to repulsion. However, Rebekka herself makes the first renunciation of their relationship; she acts out her own drama of denial.

Rebekka's renunciation is necessary because of the guilt which is present within her own consciousness. Within the structure of *Rosmersholm*, the Rosmer view of life is seen as infectious, and this disease has sickened her conception of reality. Early in the play, she responds to Kroll with the statement: "Certainly I have come to feel so much at home that I now feel almost as if I belong here, even I." Madam Helspeth speaks of the oppressiveness of Rosmersholm being like an infectious disease, a contagion, which has spread around the area from its core at Rosmersholm, and this sense of oppression is, surely, an image of guilt. The primary guilt Rebekka suffers is revealed to her by Kroll. She is not and cannot be the *child* of Rosmer's child-love, because she is not innocent. Kroll reveals to her that Dr. West, with whom she had an illicit relationship, is her father. This disclosure is indirect in the final version of *Rosmersholm*. What was blatant in the draft was subtly cloaked in the final copy of the play. The cause of Rebekka's injury is a clarification of her guilt, a final realization which affirms her renunciation of Rosmer. She makes that renunciation initially on the basis of the guilt initiated by her irrational destruction of Beate; but the motive of incest is extremely significant and this disclosure completes the destruction of the meaning of *child* in *Rosmersholm*. Rebekka, as child, was not protected by her father but injured by him. His moral emancipation is the source of her demand for freedom and the cause of her inability to assume it.

The innocence of his relationship with Rebekka is the core of Rosmer's mission. This mission is the form which his movement toward the mythical assumes. In the first place, his work is seen as the rejection of the restrictive ethic of his fathers. It is a denial of that oppression and an attempt to achieve freedom from the controlling ascetic attitude which characterizes the Rosmer view of life. It is also a demand to live a spontaneous and natural life. The essential quality of Rosmer's dream of emancipation is innocence, freedom from guilt. The temptation which came to Brand through Agnes presented itself in an assurance that together they could create a new form of man. Rebekka's temptation of Rosmer is based upon an analogous promise, the emancipation and ennoblement of mankind.

As a tangible program for social reform, however, Rosmer's mission is vague and inarticulately described. He sees himself, with Rebekka, as some kind of teacher, providing experiences in which people will determine for themselves a natural morality which is instinctive, apprehended in individual consciousness, and not imposed upon one generation by another. He outlines his task to Kroll:

ROSMER. . . . I will live and dedicate my life's work to this one thing alone—the creation of a true democracy in this country . . . I will define democracy's true task . . . to make all men in this country into noblemen, . . . by freeing their minds and purifying their will.

KROLL. You are a dreamer, Rosmer. Will you free them? Will you purify them?

ROSMER. No, dear friend, I will only awaken them to the task. Each must accomplish it for himself.

Rosmer's dream of his mission is clearly the manifestation of his desire for a freedom from imposed guilt and an ability to encompass the phenomenal without suffering. His search is for happiness, and he defines happiness as innocence. Initially Rebekka serves as an image of chaste happiness, and she is the core of his concept of a new reality—light-filled, tranquil, peaceful. Their "pure comradeship between man and woman" is the ground of his mythical notion of a purity and nobleness possible for all men. The space of time between Beate's death and Kroll's intrusion is seen by both Rebekka and Rosmer as an interlude of apparent calm and peaceful joy, an experiment in innocence:

REBEKKA. How beautiful it was when we sat there inside together, in the twilight. And we helped each other lay out our new life-plans. You were to go out into active life—today's active life, as you said. You were to go as a liberating visitor from one home to another. To win over minds and wills. To create nobleman around you, in wider and wider circles. Noble men.

ROSMER. Happy noble men. . . . For it is happiness
that ennobles, Rebekka.

Later Rosmer makes the direct equation between happiness and innocence: "that luxury of the world which
would make life so marvellously sweet to live! . . .
Peaceful, happy innocence." However, the attempt to
bring that relationship out into the public destroys its
surface tranquility and reveals the processes which are
its reality.

Brendel's two appearances in *Rosmersholm* signal the
condition of Rosmer's own state of mind. He appears at
first when it seems possible for Johannes Rosmer to free
himself from the restrictive ethic of his family, to break
loose from the "Rosmersholm view of life." Brendel announces that he is about to make his dreams take tangible shape and to put into action those ideas which up to
this point have been merely the work of his own con-
templation:

> You see, when golden dreams dropped down upon
> me—intoxicating me—when new, dizzying, far-ranging
> thoughts grew in me, carried me off on their wings,
> then I gave them form in poems, in visions, in
> pictures. In bold outline, you understand.

Brendel describes his work as existing only in fantasy;
but then for some reason, he feels the demand to realize
these dreams concretely in an act which communicates
them to others. But when Brendel does sacrifice his visions, he finds them empty and void. He appears once
again and confesses his emptiness and disillusionment at
the precise moment when Rosmer is voicing his despair,
when he reveals to Rebekka that it will be impossible for
him to fulfill the task of emancipation because he himself is no longer innocent. Brendel's discovery gives
resonance to Rosmer's own:

> Just as I am prepared to empty the horn of plenty, I
> make the painful discovery that I am bankrupt. For
> five and twenty years I have sat like a miser on his
> locked money-box. And so yesterday when I opened it

and wanted to draw forth the treasure—there was nothing there! The teeth of time had ground it all to dust. There was nothing, not anything in the whole business.

His dream is void and so is Rosmer's. However, in each of Ibsen's plays the resolution contains some sense of the disillusioned hero re-forming his myth. That desperate creative act is suggested in the ending of *Brand*, and it informs the ambiguous movement into romance in the reunion of Peer and Solveig. In *The Wild Duck* that reformation of myth is ironic; it is implicit in Relling's description of the way in which Hjalmar will use the death of Hedvig in a rhetorical plea for sympathy. In *Rosmersholm* the re-formation of myth is a complex and paradoxical movement, the first of the richly ambiguous endings which culminates in the re-creation of the avalanche in *When We Dead Awaken*.

Brendel's grotesque suggestion of Rebekka's sacrifice moves Rosmer into demanding proof of the ennoblement which Rebekka claims she has achieved. However, his conception of that sacrifice and her conception of ennoblement are difficult and complex images working within the play. He describes the sacrifice he wishes her to make:

. . . I seem to see you before my very eyes. You are standing out on the footbridge—out in the middle. Now you are leaning over the rail. Dizzy, drawn in fascination down toward the rushing water!

The language of this description relates Rosmer's concept of the suicide from the footbridge to the recurrent image of the fall into the abyss. This act is the irrational submission to a compelling temptation. The image of the rushing white horses and the rushing water are related; when Rosmer sees Beate as the image of his guilt, he cries out: "These horrible imaginings! I shall never be rid of them. I feel it, I know it. And any moment they will come rushing in upon me and bring back the thought of the dead one!" Rebekka continues: "Like the white horses of Rosmersholm." Rosmer replies: "Yes, like that. Rushing forth in the darkness—in the silence."

The white horses are both the image of the irrational energy of sexuality and the demand that the guilt which such energy causes be expiated. However, as Beate moves from an image of illusory tranquility—"there is something mild and gentle in thinking about Beate"— Rebekka moves from the victim of a strong energy, seen in the image of a storm at sea, to a strange calmness. She describes the change she has undergone to Rosmer:

> All the rest—that evil, sense-intoxicated desire—is gone, far, far away from me. All that wild energy is supressed into quiet and silence. An inner rest has fallen on me. A stillness as upon one of the cliffs where birds nest under the midnight sun at home in the north.

Rebekka uses images of energy and turbulance resolving into images of calm and rest. This resolution of irrational energy into peace describes Rebekka's personal movement from an uncontrollable sexuality into an ascetic renunciation of sexuality. Her language uses material from Ibsen's recurrent spatial metaphor. Passion is seen in the image of a storm at sea and the rushing water of the millrace—metaphors related to the abyss; the escape from passion is seen in imagery of light, stillness, and height—metaphors related to the eternal stasis of the "infinite arch of heaven." The tranquility which Rebekka describes is the absence of desire. Her sense of calm and peace is described in images which Rosmer applied to their relationship earlier, but that description has been clarified as an illusion. At this point, Rebekka declares that Rosmer has succeeded in his vocation of emancipation and ennoblement; she is now free of the demands which are the source of guilt. In her own imagination Rebekka no longer threatens his innocence since she is incapable of allowing their relationship to become a sexual one. The transformation in Rebekka from frenzy to calm is part of an essential antithesis in the play between conditions of aggressive or *wild* lust and conditions of innocence, freedom from desire. She calls that condition an "ennoblement"; but she also sees it as the manifestation of "the Rosmersholm view of life," and she has described that vision of reality as the source of injury:

> Rosmersholm has broken me . . . destroyed me completely. I had a healthy and courageous will when I came here. Now I am controlled by a strange law. From this day on, I don't feel as if I had courage for anything in the world.

Rebekka sees that transformation ambivalently—"as a great, self-denying love" which they realized in their life together and as the consequence of the view of life which has "infected" her will, leaving it with no energy, no ability to endure. Rebekka's movement into this energy-less state is a kind of death itself, related to the death-in-life Ibsen will explore in *John Gabriel Borkman* and *When We Dead Awaken*.

The tension in *Brand* and *Emperor and Galilean* between the mythical and the phenomenal is very clear. Both of these earlier heroes focus their attention upon a created form, a sense of the universe as their own imagination comprehends it. This act, however, is a renunciation of the phenomenal nature of their experience; it is ascetic in its movements away from sexuality. Phenomenal experience both tempts and repels these heroes, and one aspect of the fear of experience is the dread that erotic experience will reveal their own subjection to energies which cannot be controlled by the conscious mind. The movement toward the various myths of the comprehension of reality seems to be an effort to identify with energy or power, freeing the self from its fear of incompleteness. The movement toward the mythical is a desire for innocence, a sense of timelessness, and an inability to locate the self in the center of a comprehensible reality. Ambivalently, it is the desire to identify with reality and to be the focus of reality simultaneously.

In each of the plays which we have discussed, this personal myth has proved inadequate, and the attempt to hold it within consciousness has been a destructive act. Rebekka is the core of Rosmer's mythical vision. At the beginning of the action, Rosmer is already an apostate. He has given up his work as a clergyman because of his loss of faith, and he has reconstructed a new concept of reality based upon his apparently desireless, innocent relationship with Rebekka West. However, repeating the typical action, Rosmer's faith in his reconstructed reality disintegrates. The reality of Rebekka's sexuality is revealed, and that transformation is the primary action of the drama as an event which happens to Rosmer. Rebekka moves from being the image of form, the displacement of the basic metaphor of the "infinite arch of heaven," to being the image of formlessness in her association with the antithetical paradigm of images relating to the abyss. This transition is further complicated in Rebekka's final movement into a condition of deathlike calm and stasis in her renunciation of sexuality which is caused by her disabling guilt. However, that particular transformation is not accepted by Rosmer as a certainty, and he demands that she prove her renunciation in an actual sacrifice which reenacts Beate's suicide.

The final relationship between Rosmer and Rebekka is a strangely compelling one. Rebekka continues to identify with the image of the white horses, the mermaid, and the sea-troll, and she becomes a lure for Rosmer himself, leading him to the millrace and his death. As the idea of her suicide takes form within his imagination, he confesses "there is a fascinating horror in this—!" Rosmer, like Julian, is suspended between two halves of the world, two strategies of consciousness; and he sees both as temptations. Rebekka is the vessel of both temptations at this point which voice themselves in Rosmer's consciousness. Rosmer submits to the temptation she offers, which is a complete renunciation, but he envisions the renunciation in the image of a marriage. He acts out the formal sacrifice which is an acceptance of the mythical—the ultimate movement toward the formal; but his action is a surrender to the energy of the millrace, the attenuated metaphor of the sea and the abyss.

One aspect of the mutual suicide is the removal of the threat of sexuality. Rosmer's insistence upon her sacrifice fixes her within time in a state of innocence. Sacrificed, she will remain for him as she is—damaged by their mutual guilt for Beate's death, but, at least, untouched by their own sexual deeds. And, as well, this act will preserve Rebekka's condition of calm and rest, her "ennoblement" which is a re-created innocence. Both of them see their act as an expiation. The expiation is ambiguous since they see themselves as their own judges, free from an external ethic. Their act is, in this sense, existential. However, while the image of the white horses signals a movement within their own consciousness, they seem to be answering a demand made externally. The externality of that demand, however, appears because their movement toward the suicide is not completely willed by their conscious minds. That movement is their response to a lure, to the fascination of the rushing water and phenomenal energy. However, in the strange transformations which take place in this work, that movement provides only the illusion of phenomenality. The marriage is not a sexual action; this union exists only in the complicity of their renunciation of life.

6

The Master Builder

In 1891 Henrik Ibsen moved from Munich to Christiania (Oslo), ending his twenty-seven-year exile from Norway. He completed his final group of plays in Norway: *The Master Builder* (1892), *Little Eyolf* (1894), *John Gabriel Borkman* (1896), and *When We Dead Awaken* (1899). Although Ibsen identified his last play as a "dramatic epilogue," he did consider writing another work even after he suffered a serious stroke in the spring of 1899. However, he had a second stroke in 1901 which made that project impossible, and he never recovered sufficiently to realize that project. Ibsen died on May 23, 1906.

These final four plays comprise a related group even though Ibsen continued his experimentation with dramatic form and produced a radically different kind of structure in *When We Dead Awaken*. Ibsen agreed with Count Prozer's observation that the last play was, most clearly, an epilogue for the final series which began with *The Master Builder*.[1] The unity of this subgroup of plays is not a departure from Ibsen's basic concerns, but is, rather, the evidence of a special kind of intensification. These plays are retrospective in a way markedly different from the plays which precede them. They deal with a hero looking back over a period of time and identifying the quality of that past experience. Each of Ibsen's plays deals with a crucial recognition of the ambiguity of self-consciousness, the irreconcilable tension between the

mythical and phenomenal strategies of encompassing experience. That recognition is frequently the motive for
the hero's conscious movement toward death. The consciousness attempts to encompass phenomenal experience and yet cannot; purely phenomenal experience is
the source of guilt, the sense of process which gives a
desired object and then removes it. The last plays, however, distill the action of *Rosmersholm*. They present the
female figure who comes late to the hero's life and offers
him a second opportunity to experience an erotic relationship, under the guise of a mythical project; and yet
that temptation is not simple. The temptation offers
merely the illusion of an escape from the attenuated and
metaphoric death of their present lives; actually that
temptation reveals their disabling guilt and exposes the
fact that actual death is the only escape from that guilt.
Each of the figures—Hilde, Asta, Ella, and Irene—exposes the quality of a past eroticism with which the hero
was unable to deal; and the action of the play exposes the
injury which kept him from that erotic object and forces
him to confront that injury.

The ambiguity of the female figure is clearer in these
plays than in the preceding works. In each of these plays
Ibsen presents the typical triad: the wife who voices the
hero's guilt and the fascinating figure who tempts the
hero—the pairing of Hilde and Aline, Asta and Rita, Ella
and Gunhild, and very complexly, Maja and Irene. However, the ambiguity of the kind of relationship embodied
in Beate and Rebekka is even more focused in these
plays. These women reveal both a past erotic appeal and
the hero's rejection of eroticism. They return to tempt
again. However, the second temptation is clearly a lure
to death. In the last two plays there is a curious image of
awakening; however, that awakening is in no sense a redemptive or transcendent act. Awakening in these plays
is a metaphor of a dream of expiation through death.
Rubek's mythical image of Irene as a statue puts her in
the form of a young girl awakening from death into an
infinite innocence. The dream of awakening is motivated

by the confrontation with guilt. In each play, there is an ambiguous use of the image of *child* which was subtly present in *Rosmersholm*. The condition of childhood is the embodiment of the innocence, the freedom from sexuality and guilt which is desired; however, each play has injured and dead children which stand as images of guilt: Solness's dead infant sons; the figure of Eyolf himself— with dead staring eyes looking up from the depths of the sea; Ella Rentheim's unborn children; and the strange injured child of the statue in *When We Dead Awaken*. These images are all present in earlier plays, but the use of the child is a clearer aspect of Ibsen's dramatic structure in these last plays. This study does not deal with *Little Eyolf*, but I would refer readers to James Keran's revealing discussion of this play.[2]

The Master Builder is Ibsen's clearest statement of his basic paradox; and the strange image of Hilde Wangel standing in curious triumph as she continues to salute the figure of Halvard Solness, the master builder—who no longer stands atop the tower but lies dead below in the quarry—personifies that paradox. At this final moment, Hilde is celebrating her success and, in a sense, she is also retreating from the reality of Solness's death, putting aside the recognition that the triumph of the master builder is also his destruction.

Hilde's bizarre appearance and manner give her a distinct, if equivocal, identity within the structure of characters. However, Hilde is most clearly significant as she clarifies Solness's own will—as she projects his desires, reveals his fear, and defines the nature of his action. The integrity of the Solness-Hilde relationship makes it impossible to discuss the quality of one character apart from the relationship itself. In order to discuss the nature of Solness's action it is necessary to deal with the problematic Hilde Wangel and all associated with her as a paradigm within the consciousness of the master builder himself. Her presence makes vital and tangible what is repressed or latent in his imagination and releases the energy which makes his paradoxical ascent possible. Indeed, Halvard Solness's action of climbing the tower of his newly constructed home to hang the ceremonial wreath is the fulfillment of Hilde's vision of him.

It is important to understand Solness's emotional condition when Hilde arrives at his home. At this point, Solness and Doctor Herdal are discussing the master builder's fortunate career. The exposition is given on two levels: the factual in which the details of Solness's success are enumerated and the emotional in which his reactions to these events are implied. Two fears which seem to be acutely suffered by Solness are implicit in this conversation: his strong dread of youthful competition which has been directly manifested in his devious exploitation of Ragnar Brovik and his strange guilt which is projected in his bewildered reaction to the events which seem to answer his own unvoiced desires. The guilt is, clearly, a fear of recrimination. Immediately after Solness expresses this fear to Herdal, Hilde arrives:

SOLNESS.   Changes are coming. I suspect it. And I feel them approaching. Some one will begin to demand: "Step back for me!" And so all the others will storm after him, imitating him and crying: "Give way—give way—give way!" Just you watch, Doctor. In time youth will come here and knock upon the door. . . . [and] then it is the end of master builder Solness. (A *knock upon the door.*)

Hilde provides the visible form of Halvard's own fear, and the ambiguity of that fear informs his attraction to Hilde. She provides the object both of his own attraction to youth and his fear that the younger generation will destroy his identity as *bygmester* as he destroyed Brovik. She is, in this sense, the energy of youth which he desires to regain.

Hilde's relationship with Solness is analogous to Rebekka's relationship with Rosmer, although in *Rosmersholm* the union of the two figures has a more realistic base. The relationship in *The Master Builder* is explained rationally, but Ibsen removes that relationship from a phenomenal ground in two important ways. First of all, the mystery or equivocation of that original incident in Lysanger remains vague and unspecified, and, secondly, the future of their relationship is conceived in terms of fantasy. Hilde's revelation of the event at Lysanger is a typical revelation of the past, but Ibsen does not clarify the reality of this memory; the event remains equivocal. What is significant, however, is the emotional quality of Hilde's remembering and the ways in which it stirs the latent energies in Solness's imagination:

HILDE. There was music in the churchyard. And many, many hundreds of people. We schoolgirls were dressed in white. And we all had flags as well. . . . Then you climbed up over the scaffold-ing. Straight up to the very top. And you had a great wreath with you, and you hung the wreath high up on the weather vane. . . . It was so mar-velously thrilling to stand there and look up at you. To think if he should fall off! He—the master builder himself!

SOLNESS (*as if to divert her*). Yes, yes, yes. That might well have happened. For one of those white clad devil-children—she carried on so and cried up to me—

HILDE (*beaming in joy*). "Hurray for master builder Solness."

SOLNESS. —and waved and swung her flag at me— so that I almost became dizzy from looking at it.

HILDE (*softly, seriously*). That devil-child—it was *I*. . . . For it was so terribly beautiful and thrilling.

In Hilde's imagination Solness's deed at Lysanger was magnificent because it was the fulfillment of aspiration and because it was accomplished, in her opinion, without fear. The very impossibility of the task of climbing to the top of the tower gives her a sense of the deed as mythical:

I could not conceive that anyone could find another master builder in the whole world who could build such an enormously high tower. And then that you should stand at the very top yourself!

Hilde then pairs this vision of the ascent with a description of his *actual* deed: "But then—afterward—the *real thing happened.*" The real deed in Hilde's sense is an erotic encounter between the adult master builder and herself as an adolescent child:

> Then you said that I was beautiful in my white dress. And that I looked like a little princess. . . . And then you said that when I grew up, I should be *your* princess. . . . Then you said that you would come again in ten years, like a troll, and carry me away. To Spain or some such place. And you would buy a kingdom for me, you promised. . . . [then] You held me and kissed me, Master Builder Solness. . . . Yes, indeed, you did. You held me in both arms and bent my head back and kissed me. Many times.

Initially Hilde's revelation of this meeting is puzzling to Solness, but as the scene resolves, he senses that event as the source of a painful confusion in his own memory: "Isn't it strange?—The more I think about it now—the more it seems as if I have gone through long years torturing myself with . . . with remembering something, something like that experience, which it seems to me I must have forgotten." He sees Hilde, a figure from the moment of his triumph, as a means of confronting the threat of youth. When Solness speaks of the old sagas in which the Vikings invaded foreign lands, killing the men and carrying off the women, Hilde responds: "I think it must have been thrilling . . . to be captured." Almost immediately after that, Hilde emphasizes the vigorous conscience of such men—in Solness's terms, their freedom from guilt. And then, the young girl confesses her love of Solness and, thinly disguised, her willingness to have a sexual experience with him, the man whom the devils have chosen for her.

Ibsen has focused a complex of Solness's energies in the equivocal figure of Hilde Wangel: fear, guilt, and a tautly restrained eroticism. Hilde and Solness share the fiction of her as a beautiful princess being carried off to an imaginary kingdom. This fantasy is an illusion used by both figures, one of their mutual creating. The quality of the "kingdom" becomes of increasing importance to the hero's experience in Ibsen's play. Hilde clarifies that the particular nature of this kingdom need not be actuality. The incident at Lysanger ten years earlier is deliberately clouded, and the quality of the experience is never specifically defined as the memory of an actual event, a fantasy, a lie, or a delusion. Hilde's past relationships with Herdal and Aline are recent and clearly recalled by the others, and it seems to be a part of Ibsen's conscious design that, to them, Hilde has a specific history as a human being. To Solness, Hilde is, certainly, a tangible object; but she is—within his own imagination—a presence which he wills to be with him, a figure related to fantasy and dream. The location of their fantastic kingdom is within their own relationship. Their troubled discussion of the recurrent dream which they both share has a telling relationship to the fantasy of that kingdom. Hilde has spent the night in one of the Solness's three empty nurseries. Developing the ambiguity of the metaphor *child*, Solness finds her presence there curiously appropriate. He asks her if she has dreamed during the night:

HILDE.   Yes, indeed. But it was horrible . . . for I dreamed that I fell from a terrifyingly high, steep precipice. Do you ever dream of something like that?

SOLNESS.   Yes, I do—once in a while—

HILDE.   It is so very thrilling—when you fall and fall.

SOLNESS.   It feels as cold as ice, it seems to me.

HILDE.   Do you tuck your feet up under you while it lasts?

SOLNESS.   As high as I can bear.

Here the association of the dream and the fall is disguised but clearly evident. Perhaps the most important aspect of this dream is that it is both feared and desired: it is "thrilling," exhilarating, and yet "horrid," something which turns one cold. It is a dream, a fantasy, a recurrent withdrawal from reality with suggestions of regression. In a sense, the actual fall is also such a fantasy—both for Hilde and Solness. The fall from the tower is "horrid"; it is an experience which is feared, but the thought of it is thrilling both to the master builder and the young girl.

It is undeniable that the ascent is acutely feared by Halvard Solness. He suffers dizziness in high places. Aline reminds him that it is impossible for him to go out on the second-story balcony of his own home. The deed is, in Solness's own terms, *impossible*. And yet, he once accomplished it. The fear which he suffers in high places is defined, through metaphor, as conscience; he fears recrimination. The height of the tower is a freedom from obligation to others, a boundless self-satisfaction, a sense of the will as ultimate agency. Bound by his fear of recrimination, Solness fears the act which would assert his freedom from obligation. The ascent, in one sense, is the tangible exercise of a creative fantasy held by Solness and Hilde—the denial of his actual work and the affirmation of an illusory dream vocation:

SOLNESS. . . . nothing actually built, and nothing sacrificed to get anything built, either. Nothing, nothing—the whole thing!

HILDE. And you will never build anything again?

SOLNESS (*energetically*). I am just beginning at this very moment.

HILDE. What then? What then? Tell me immediately!

SOLNESS. The only thing which I believe can accommodate human joy—I will build that now.

HILDE. Master Builder, now you mean our castles in the air.

SOLNESS. Castles in the air, yes.

HILDE.   I am afraid that you will grow dizzy before we climb halfway.

SOLNESS.   Not if I can go hand in hand with *you*, Hilde.

In Solness's own imagination there is a puzzling ambiguity between dream, or fantasy, and its tangible manifestation in experience. Ibsen projects this ambiguity through Solness's conception of a will which calls and is answered—in the presence of Kaja, in the burning of Aline's home, and in the presence of Hilde. He sees the fulfilling of his own desires as a supernatural answering of something demonic in his nature over which he has no rational control. The actual ascent is complicated by Solness's confused sense of will.

Solness envisions the final ascent as a re-creation of the first triumph: ". . . then I will come down and take her in my arms and kiss her . . . many, many times." Certainly it is significant that Solness anticipates a repetition of the paired incidents at Lysanger. Again the impossible and the erotic are joined, and it is an important factor in the paradoxical resolution of this modern tragedy that the repetition of the extraordinary climb is destructive. The climb is an assertion only in an ambiguous sense; unconsciously the ascent is a willed suicide, a surrender to recrimination motivated by guilt, and Hilde destroys that which she would have.

Early in the play Solness and Aline expose their guilt, each using the other to sustain the pain of that guilt. Solness bears an acute guilt for the destruction of Aline's home—not only the physical structure but her *home* in the sense of family structure. Aline explores the quality of her guilt, a shame for her sorrow which, as it is revealed, so weakened her in her grief at the loss of the family home that her nursing children were made ill. The quality of the marriage is barren: it is childless, without hope, sustained only by guilt.

Solness considers the fire which destroyed Aline's family home as the manifestation of his own will—if not the actual cause, the result of an energy released in his own unvoiced desire. The "infinite debt" which he owes Aline is associated with the fire as the destruction of her very being, her vocation as mother:

> . . . her life's work had to be burned up, it was crushed, smashed to pieces—so that mine could gain a kind of great victory. Yes, for you shall see that Aline had a gift for building, she too . . . for building the souls of little children, Hilde. For building children's souls in such a way that they were formed in a noble, beautiful way. So that they would mature into upright and full human souls.

Yet in a grotesque absurdity, Ibsen clarifies that Solness's guilt is based upon a misapprehension of Aline's own nature. Aline herself suffers from a guilt which is, in a sense, more rationally derived than that of her husband. Her grief, still acutely strong, is not caused primarily by the loss of her sons, but, rather, by the loss of the house and its contents—most painfully by the destruction of her dolls:

> All the old portraits on the walls were burned. And all the old silk dresses were burned. They had belonged to my family for years and years. And all of mother's and grandmother's lacework—it was burned as well. And think—the jewelry there! (*oppressively*) And all the dolls. . . . I had nine beautiful dolls. . . . it was so painful for me, so very painful for me. . . .they were all burned, alas. There was no one who thought of saving them. O, it is so tragic to think about it.

Aline speaks to Hilde of her life with the dolls, a fantasy which continued after her marriage in secret play hid from Solness: "For, you see, in a way, there was life in them too. I carried them under my heart. As if they were little unborn children." Aline does not mourn the loss of a vocation realized in creative motherhood, but she does suffer from the destruction of a regressive fantasy which allowed her to retreat from the responsibilities of her actual life. Her emotional insistence upon duty, upon responsibility, certainly derives from the tension between this retreat or regression, and her accommodation of the present. But, ironically, that guilt which Solness bears so painfully is one which is a product of his own imagination. The action which is the source of that guilt is actually Aline's renunciation, not his; her retreat into fantasy was an escape from the demands of her real function as mother. Aline's unwholesome adult play with the dolls reveals her true nature. Her real grief for those lifeless toys which were invested with life only in her imaginative play is the cause of the death of her actual children, the twin boys. Rather than nourishing them with her milk, she—made ill in sorrow—poisoned them. And, it is significant to note, she insisted upon fulfilling her duty, upon feeding them with her own milk, despite her illness. This barren implementation of duty is the enactment of a painful guilt, an insistent rehearsal of expiation.

The Master Builder is undeniably an exploration of guilt. In different ways both Solness and Aline disguise their guilt in conceiving of their sons' death as the operation of God's will, mysterious and not to be questioned. Solness's guilt, as well, expresses itself in his concept of *luck*, his own awareness that his position has been reached through the exploitation of others, conscious or unconscious.

> Who called the helpers or servers? It was *I*! And so they came and surrendered to my will. . . . It was what good people call having good fortune. But I will tell you how it feels to have such luck! It is like having a great raw wound in one's breast. And the helpers and servers flay the skins of other men to try and close *my* wound! —But the wound never heals. Never— never! And if only you knew how it can sometimes ache and burn.

Halvard Solness's guilt is both a painful realization that his action has damaged others and a critical fear that such exploitation will be suffered by him in turn. However, his own guilt must not be minimized. He senses that his will is an energy which is uncontrolled; his will is answered even thought it is not voiced.

The ambiguity of will and vocation in *The Master Builder* is crucial to an understanding of the play. In Solness's own consciousness the relationship between will and vocation is equivocal. Here, perhaps, is the primary source of obscurity in the play itself. Solness claims that initially he conceived of his work as the celebration of his devotion to God; and yet he is in profound despair as he realizes that he is subject to those energies within himself which he cannot control—those trolls which call, successfully, upon those who help and serve. Early in his career Solness understood his vocation to be the focal point of his love of God; and yet, in the critical incident of the fire, he realized his vocation was the extension of his own will. His unvoiced will seems realized in the coming to reality of his fantasy of the burning house. His freedom from the will of God which demands such a sacrifice is won, in his imagination, through the ascent of the tower at Lysanger. Solness rejects the concept of a determining God in his effort to see himself as complete; and yet he is unable to confront those aspects of his being which are not controlled by his conscious mind. That inability manifests itself in his concept of the *troll* within him. The troll is an image which externalizes his own irrationality. In this sense, this declaration of freedom from God is an attempt to purge himself of that aspect of his own will which he sees as destructive and exploitative. Solness reports his denial of God to Hilde: "Hear me now, right here, Mighty One. Hereafter I will be a free master builder, I too. In my domain. As you in yours. I will never again build churches for you. Only homes for people." The death of the children became for him the image of sacrifice, the deprivation of his own love; and he wills himself to build houses for the happiness of others. His vocation then still exists as the focusing of love—that is, as directed away from the self, but even this comes to nothing, and—with Hilde—he directs his vocation to fantasy.

Hilde's freedom from guilt—"her robust consciousness"—is a clarification of Solness's own desire to be free from his sense of human obligation. Hilde's strength, of course, is her youth—that which Solness fears (as competition) and that for which he longs (freedom from guilt). In the metaphors of the play, Hilde is both of the sea and the mountains. As in all of Ibsen's uses of the metaphors of sea and height, the freedom which Hilde promises is an illusion of freedom, not an actual quality of being. She is part of the complex paradigm focused upon the image of the ascent and the heights; she seems to offer Solness freedom from the restriction and oppression of his present condition in a re-creation of some moment of freedom from the past. The freedom which Hilde offers her master builder is death: drowning in the depths and falling from the heights. To be free from guilt is to be young again, and the return to youth is an inversion of life: that is the inescapable fact of Ibsen's drama. Guilt in *The Master Builder* may be a perversion of responsibility, an unhealing wound, but in his guilt Solness does have a sense of human obligation which allows him to direct his will, to focus his energy in the realization of his vocation even though it has no tangible object. Hilde provides an object for his erotic energy, but the threat she poses, the fantasy of freedom, is ultimately destructive.

Guilt in *The Master Builder* has a strange quality. It is a painful realization of the suffering of others, and in that realization there is a sense of a human relationship, a sense of obligation and care. And yet, the presence of guilt in this play seems to carry with it a painful understanding that this sense of human obligation has made it impossible to fulfill desire. The ascent of the tower is the illusion of retreating from this reality, from the reality of obligation and guilt; but that illusion is impossible to maintain, and Solness is brought down to the earth and his death.

This play contains the typical structure of a male confronted by two conflicting female influences. The polarization illuminates a tension present within the consciousness of Solness himself. Hilde, of course, seems to be the emanation of Solness's desire to be free from guilt, to possess a pure will whose energy may be used in any action desired; Aline functions as the outward symbol of his fettered conscience, his confused and resentful apprehension of responsibility. Aline's barren submission to duty, the desiccated altruism of social gesture which equates the protocol of a visit with the need of a hysterical husband, is analogous to Solness's displaced will as he exercises the false charity of building homes to contain the happiness of others. The action which is the source of Solness's guilt is Aline's own renunciation; her retreat into fantasy as an escape from the demands of her real function.

Although Hilde does project Solness's desire for the constancy of youth, undecaying and untiring energy, he also sees her in the metaphor of the *rovfugl*, the bird of prey. This telling reference, which takes us back to the image of the falcon-female in *Brand*, focuses our imagination upon the destructiveness of Hilde's behavior. In one sense Hilde drives Solness to make that impossible ascent. Like the falcon, Hilde pursues her prey, but she is both the erotic temptation and the instrument which offers release from its threat. Also, it is Hilde who insists that Solness comment upon Ragnar's drawings, recognizing his worth in some tangible way. Ostensibly Hilde has him accomplish this task in order to bring peace to the dying Brovik. However, in that sense the deed is futile since the old man is unconscious by the time the drawings reach him. The deed is primarily significant to Solness as a confrontation with the threat of youth. Ragnar—the focus of Solness's fears—is associated with Hilde in a very interesting way. Solness confesses to Hilde: "Someday Ragnar Brovik will knock me to the earth. Crush me—as I did his father." It is significant that Ragnar himself announces the death of the master builder and that he uses images which seem drawn from Solness's own fear: "He must be smashed. Killed on the spot." Solness's final action is as much a realization of this fear as it is a deliberate act. The bringing to earth, the crushing of the master builder, is the triumph of Ragnar, the future master builder. Despite the antipathy between Hilde and Ragnar, she is the agent of his triumph. Ragnar's dismissal comes with Solness's approval of the drawings, an action insisted upon by Hilde. In one sense, Solness wills his own destruction from this point. The commitment to freedom, expressed in climbing the tower, is, paradoxically, an acceptance of his own failure and his submission to the retribution of Ragnar's triumph. The ascent is both an assertion of the will and, at the same time, a surrender to youth, a submission to an ethic which he feels wills his destruction. The ascent has the quality of a willed assertion *and* a surrender. To interpret the action as purely one or the other is to rid the play of its density and, hence, profundity.

The scope of the protagonist's task in Ibsen's last plays is significant. Consider Allmer's work on the definition of human responsibility and Rubek's "Resurrection." The awesome scope of these projects clarifies the significance of the will in Ibsen's imagination, however futile the action of those protagonists. Solness's vocation seems to be an attempt to sense form in human experience, to witness an order and to affirm meaning in life itself. He originally builds to celebrate his religious faith; but, then, that faith shattered, he builds in order to provide an environment which could contain happiness. The metaphoric depth of his vocation needs to be sounded. The two kinds of building need to be contrasted. First there is the tower which celebrated the ideal, the reality of a beneficent God. Afterward, there is the home which exists for human happiness, for the joy of family life as the primary value. First the presence of a beneficent God is destroyed in Solness's imagination; and then, in his relationship with Aline, the possibility of a creative union with another human being is destroyed. The new home which Solness builds combines both structures: the tower and the home—both imitations of a form and inner order which Solness comes to realize are nonexistent in his experience. There is no happiness in the Solness home which the new house could contain, and he seeks the ideal of a creative relationship in the illusion he shares with Hilde.

Ibsen defines Solness's triumph, the fulfillment of his will in the act of hanging the wreath on the tower, as the creation of an illusion. The assertion of his will is the building of an imaginary kingdom; and the illusion is sustained, despite the reality of the fall, in the imagination of Hilde Wangel as she stares at the place of Solness's triumph crying: "My—my master builder!" The characterization of Hilde is a complex substructure within the complete play which clarifies the quality of Solness's fear of youth, the kind of retreat into illusion which that fear demands, and the destructiveness of such a distorted accommodation of experience. And yet, the energy of that wish—that the self should be continually renewed in vigorous creativity—is certainly given value in the play despite its destructiveness.

However, those who read the resolution of *The Master Builder* as a triumph of idealism, assertion realized in action, are blinded to the essential hysteria of the tragic event. Solness's action is the fulfillment of his own sense of recrimination; it is a willed expiation, a regressive withdrawal from the pain of guilt. The creation of illusionary castles is somewhat analogous to the perverted play of a married woman who treats her dolls as it they were real children and grieves more for their loss than she does for her real sons. Ironically, each of the two females who clarify Solness's personal conflict offers him a retreat from actual experience: Hilde moves Solness toward the creation of *luftslottene*, castles in the air, erotic phantasms; and Aline reveals her own precious illusions, her childish play which was a rehearsal in fantasy of actions she would not or could not put into practice in the reality of her own experience. Aline offers Solness a continuation of their barren, attenuated life. Evasions of a direct confontation with experience are persistent in this play. And the suicide itself has both the quality of a confrontation and a retreat.

The Master Builder is an imitation of a human being unable to relate to any person beyond himself, unable to apprehend a satisfying object either for his erotic energy or for the ideal of his own creative ability. Unable to deal with reality, the main figures in *The Master Builder* retreat into a variety of illusions. The most vital illusion, of course, is the imaginary kingdom which Solness and his Hilde build and to which Solness ascends. The ascent into illusion is also, however, a suidical fall, a submission to an ethic of recrimination. While the act affirms a freedom of the will, it renounces life; and the final focus of *The Master Builder* is upon the figure of Hilde Wangel as she attempts to maintain a dream of the master builder at the top of the tower, unable to accept the reality of the dead figure below in the quarry. The presence of Hilde on the stage at this final moment is significant. Hilde has been the source of Solness's final concept of form, and he has created a personal myth on the ground of their relationship. However, that form is fantasy and vulnerable to the tangible demands of phenomenal reality. That fantasy only pretends to encompass the phenomenal as it celebrates the erotic; it is actually an escape from the sexuality of the relationship, and to avoid that threat, Solness destroys the possibility that the relationship could be sexual by destroying himself, by doing "the impossible." The image of form which is Hilde's dream of a free and strong conscience, of sexuality free from guilt and the fear of process, dissolves once again, and the abyss—here the crushing reality of the quarry—claims its victim.

7

When We Dead Awaken

Although *When We Dead Awaken* looks back to earlier works, the play also moves forward toward a new concept of dramatic form as Ibsen extends the form of the realistic plays but is freer to explore the metaphors of mental process without tying them to a plausible or naturalistic base. In the earlier realistic plays, such as *Ghosts* and *The Wild Duck*, Ibsen distributed the detail which informed the primary tension throughout the surface texture of the play, and while the metaphoric use of scenic elements such as the darkness, cold, and dampness of the northern region in *Ghosts* is obviously related to the sense of man as victim that the play presents, the single detail is not overriding. The individual detail is part of a dense surface texture which operates upon the spectator. Also, in *The Wild Duck* the clear metaphoric uses of photography and retouching are obvious but not predominant, and they work with a whole paradigm of realistic details to suggest concepts related to seeing, recording truth, creating artifice, and the reforming of images themselves. In *The Master Builder, Little Eyolf,* and *John Gabriel Borkman,* there is sufficient detail to give the illusion of the play as realistic, but the characters in these plays are consumed by their immediate acts and the plays concentrate upon a crucial event without attempting to suggest the processes of daily life in a distribution of detail to the degree of the earlier plays. Consequently, the metaphoric quality of such images as building is clearer and more a part of our conscious response to the play. Therefore, we identify the plays as more symbolic and less realistic, despite the fact that the earlier plays are just as metaphoric in quality. In these later plays the metaphoric structure is revealed as closer to our conscious perception of the play.

In *When We Dead Awaken*, the process of concentration which marks the difference between *The Wild Duck* and *The Master Builder* produces a disarmingly simplified play. Almost no detail exists in *When We Dead Awaken* which does not directly relate to a very distilled inner structure. That inner structure itself is ambiguous, but it is not elaborately distributed throughout a thick layer of surface detail. The play has been criticized as weak and inadequate, a product of Ibsen's failing imagination—primarily, I think, because it violates our expectations of what a play written by Henrik Ibsen will be. *When We Dead Awaken* contains the story which Ibsen inevitably tells, but the form of that narrative is different even though it is a logical extension of his previous method. The world which is created in *When We Dead Awaken* is nothing more than a metaphoric space. It is not an abstraction, but it contains only those aspects of nature which have meaning for the characters who perform this drama; it is the environment they need in order to explore the tension between their conscious experience and those aspects of their being which rebel against the form that their conscious experience assumes. The environment of *When We Dead Awaken* is a reduced imaginative field which, for Ibsen, clarifies the tension between two opposing strategies of consciousness. The external action of the play moves simply through this reduced scene. Rubek, a sculptor who is no longer young, returns to the place of his youth with his young wife, Maja. At the spa where they are staying he meets a strange woman who is traveling with a sister of mercy. He recognizes her as Irene, the woman who posed for his masterpiece, "The Resur-

rection Day," and disappeared when the work was near-
ing completion. She reveals that she left him because he
never touched her even though their work together demanded that she expose herself to him completely. After
leaving him, she lived a dissolute life. He feels that he
needs her since he has produced nothing of value since
that masterpiece. Rubek's wife is attracted to a sportsman, Ulfheim, and goes off hunting with him. Irene
and Rubek climb the mountain toward the heights. The
four meet, and Irene and Rubek climb further into a
storm while the other two descend to the forest. An
avalanche kills the sculptor and his model.

The complexity of the play derives from the density
of the image of Irene. The tangible figure of Irene, as
a character on the stage, is the stimulating image of a
complex series of antitheses which form the basic tension of Rubek's consciousness: the presence of this
strangely injured woman opposes the absence of the
statue—its internment in the grave vaults of the mu-
seum; her transformation in the processes of time opposes the suspension of her youth in the fixed time of
the statue; her present death-in-life opposes the vitality
of her youth caught in the statue; the hardness of the
marble opposes the softness of the real woman; the suspended innocence of the statue opposes the sordid
reality of her experience. These antitheses are clear, but
an analogy is also at work: both Irene and the statue are
conceived as dead, and the phenomenal reality of Irene
as a sexual object exists only as memory, stimulating
Rubek's sexuality but only as an imitation of a past
eroticism. The stage character, Irene, dressed in white to
suggest the dead quality of the marble statue in which
Rubek re-created her form, is only the signal of the
complexity of the processes of consciousness embodied
in Rubek's imaginative conception of her. It is necessary
to explore that complexity.

Rubek defines his conception of that statue:

I wanted to create that pure woman in the form in
which I saw her awakening on Resurrection Day. Not

astonished at anything new or unfamiliar or unimagined, but filled with a sacred joy as she discovers
herself again—unchanged—she, the woman of the
earth—in the higher, freer, happier regions—after
the long dreamless sleep of death.

It would be possible to describe the action of most of
Ibsen's plays as either the exhaustion of forms or the
disintegration of concepts of reality. The plays end with
their heroes embracing a myth of form, an illusion of a
self-determining reality when all other illusions of form
are spent. In *When We Dead Awaken* the artist figure
is tired and disillusioned, clinging very weakly to a concept of himself as an artist. The masterwork has been
completed. That work does attempt to formalize a concept of reality, but it attempts to fix in time that which
cannot be made static. Reality is process and that process
cannot be halted. While the work itself was *in process*, it
offered satisfaction for Rubek; but once it is completed,
the discrepancy between it, the formal concrete embodiment of what he wishes reality to be, and his perception
of what actually exists becomes clear to him. He does
alter the composition to meet the demands of that
reality, but the work ceases to satisfy.

I had a year or a year and a half of loneliness and
brooding and put the last—the very last touch on my
work. "The Resurrection Day" was received all over
the world and brought me fame—and all other splen-
dors besides. (*With more warmth.*) But I did not
love my own work any longer. Men's bouquets and
praises drove me nauseated and despairing into the
thickest forest.

The creation of the statue is a means of achieving his
sexual object without guilt, but the creation of a mythical image to substitute for experience does not continue
to satisfy. What Rubek has done, of course, is to elect
a substitute for Irene in Maja and live a life of indolence
and comfort. But the formlessness of this unshaped life
—in which he cannot determine his reality as the em-

bodiment of his own imagination—is frustrating to him. That frustration is evident in his declaration: "There is still a certain happiness in being able to feel free and unfettered at all sides. To have everything which you could dream of having. Everything external, that is."

After the completion of "The Resurrection Day" Rubek only models portrait busts—works for which he is highly paid and which, in themselves, project a concept of reality. They are a bestiary, reflecting the animal-like qualities of their subjects:

> On the surface there is that "striking likeness," which it is called, and which some people stare and gape at so astonished — (*lowers his voice*) —but in their inner core they are respectable, honest horse-faces and obstinate donkey-snouts and droop-eared, low-browed dog-skulls and swollen pig-heads —and slack, brutal boar-likenesses sometimes as well.

While the initial version of his masterpiece attempted to transcend reality and create its own world, its modification and the portrait work, the product of his "un-shaped" life, deals with reality on its own terms, mimetically and not romantically. The modification of the statue which Rubek makes after Irene's departure is critical. He describes its amplifications to Irene:

> I re-created that which I saw around me in the world with my eyes. I had to include it—I couldn't otherwise, Irene. I widened the plinth—so that it would be wide and spacious. And upon it I laid a section of the curving, bursting earth. And up from the crevices in the earth there now swarm men and women with hidden animal faces. Women and men—as I knew them from life.

The symbolism of this revised sculpture is significant. Rubek makes Irene, the image of purity, secondary to the demonic, sensual figures before her and positions himself, washing his hands clean in the stream before her, a man burdened with guilt, who cannot free himself completely from the earth crust. I call him remorse over a forfeited life. He sits there and dips his fingers in the rippling water—to wash them pure—and he is gnawed and tortured by the thought that he will never, never succeed.

The relationship between Rubek and Irene is integral to Rubek's own sense of being, the realization of his identity. The statue is the manifestation of both Rubek's and Irene's desire; the movement to encompass what *child* means is shared by them. Irene's quest is to seek out and find the child. That statue in her imagination is the creation of their individual wills in an imaginative union: "My whole soul—you and I—we, we, we and our child were in that lonely image." Rubek's desire is to re-create that union as he asks Irene: "Be one with me in all my striving." Within the complete play of meanings in *When We Dead Awaken* the act of identifying with the fixed and unchanging image of the statue —with the deliberate illusion—denies the reality of Rubek's and Irene's own sexuality; and the consequence is the metaphoric death of the title of the play.

Irene is the the temptation which leads Rubek into the heights. She provides the temptation to abandon art (form or myth) for experience, and yet her sexuality is the very subject of Rubek's search for form. Irene is the final figure in the series of women who come to the Ibsen hero to destroy him. She is related to Hilde and Rebekka—the unexpected young woman who comes to the man late in his career and offers herself to him, apparently giving him a second chance for a successful erotic life. However, Irene also stands with Agnes, Beate, Aline as the image of the *dead wife*, the tangible manifestation of the hero's guilt. In denying them as women, the Ibsen heroes have, in a sense, killed them. They are the focus for the heroes' guilt which ambiguously derives from the eroticism they inspire and the effect which their denial of that eroticism has upon them.

Looking at the Ibsen triad in the typical way, seeing the two women in terms of the poles of freedom and responsibility, it is possible to distort their roles and the meaning of the plays in which they function. For example, we have seen that Rebekka's relationship with Beate is crucial to an understanding of that work; both women have threatened Rosmer with a risk of sexuality. Rosmer suffers guilt for his rejection of Beate, and, as well, Rubek is forced to confront the guilt he bears for his denial of Irene. In *Rosmersholm*, the demanding presence of the woman is visualized in the image of the white horses—a demand which is abstracted in the final image of Rebekka in the white shawl. In *When We Dead Awaken*, the image which in *Rosmersholm* embraced both Beate and Rebekka is concentrated in Irene who, dressed in white, conceives of herself as risen from the dead. Hilde, as well, was dressed in white when she first tempted her master builder; and she waves Aline's white shawl, distracting him, when he makes his fatal ascent of the tower.

These women, clothed in virginal white, lure their men to destruction. Each has been sacrificed, in some sense, and each demands a sacrifice which works toward the expiation of the initial crime against them. This sacrifice, which is an expiation, accomplishes in a paradoxical way what the earlier sacrifice could not: it acts out the realization of the will of the hero even if that acting out is the creation of a deliberate illusion. These women seem to be a projection of the hero's sexuality, a sexuality which they attempt to deny, but which breaks forth eventually in a destructive release of energy. They are clearly seen in the image of birds of prey—the specific metaphor assigned to Agnes and Hilde; to confront them is to be consumed by them.

Images of the processes of death, awakening, and resurrection are central to the meaning of this play. Various definitions of death, literal and figurative, are assigned in *When We Dead Awaken*. Ulfheim, the bear hunter, discusses the sculptor's material as dead and, interestingly, as willing itself to be dead and acutely resisting life: ". . . for the stone has something to struggle for too. It is dead, and wills with force and power not to let itself be hammered into life." Irene describes the experience of her death-in-life:

> I was dead for many years. They came and bound me. Tied my arms together behind my back. Then they lowered me into a grave chamber with iron bars in front of the opening. And with padded walls—so that no one on the earth above could hear the shrieks from the grave. But now I am beginning, in a way, to be resurrected from the dead.

Here are two conflicting perspectives toward death: the sense of a being resisting awakening or being forced to awaken, willing its own unchanged condition; and the sense of being forced unwillingly into restriction, constraint, darkness. In Rubek's vision of "The Resurrection Day," death is seen as a means of overcoming change: "I wanted to create that pure woman in the form in which I saw her awakening on the Resurrection Day. Not astonished at anything new or unfamiliar or unimagined, but filled with a sacred joy as she discovers herself again—unchanged—she the woman of the earth—in the higher, freer, happier region—after the long, dreamless sleep of death." Rubek's notion of death is as a means of purifying, fixing innocence, protecting from sexuality—and that "dreamless" death is peaceful, unlike Irene's vision or recollection of her metaphoric death as a frightening imprisonment.

The relationship of the statue to the concept of *child* and *childhood* is crucial. Irene conceives of the statue as a child, the creation of both herself and Rubek; she also describes her time with Rubek as the re-creation of childhood: "To go with you was the resurrection of my childhood." For both Rubek and Irene the time spent creating the statue—the three or four years—has been associated with childhood, a period of innocence in which sexuality is present but unrealized. Rubek's desire is to fix that period, to suspend that "unsullied" innocence in time; the creation of the statue is the establishment of the mythical in consciousness. It is indeed associated with death because it is a suspending of process; but it is a concept of death as benevolent, a prelude to a purified life in which one awakes transfigured, unthreatened by sexuality. She sees the denial of her actual sexuality as killing her, and she uses the actual word, *sacrifice*:

> IRENE.   When I had served you with my soul and with my body—when the statue stood completed —our child as you called it—then I laid at your feet the most valuable sacrifice by annihilating myself for all time.
>
> RUBEK (*bows his head*).   And laying my life waste.
>
> IRENE (*suddenly flaring up*).   It was just that I wanted! Never, never, never should you create anything more—after you had created that, our only child.

The sacrifice in *When We Dead Awaken* assumes a different form in this strange and reduced play. It is not a sacrifice which claims the virtual life of its victim; but rather, it is more clearly a metaphor of the renunciation of sexuality. Rubek sacrifices Irene, killing her vitality and figurative life in a denial of her function as a woman. In the metaphor of the play the real Irene is sacrificed to the statue; life is sacrificed to art. But the antithesis is not as patent as that statement suggests. The statue itself, "The Resurrection Day," is an image of innocence maintained. The completed statue fixes the purity of Irene in time, distilling her innocence, renouncing her erotic nature and the sensuality of Rubek himself. Art, form, poetry in this conception is the fixing of innocence, the reawakening to the childhood state which is, in itself, an escape from the erotic. The transition from the erotic to the ascetic is a recurrent movement in the play. Rubek describes their mutual work as an act of worship, an act in which Irene threw herself with "saintlike passion." Rubek clarifies the sense of ecstasy in that experience: the celebration of the beautiful, naked body re-created in the statue—that body whose "loveliness" put Rubek "under . . . a spell." The experience, however, was transposed in their imaginations from a sexual one to an ascetic one: from sexual experience to an act of worship, from sexual passion to a "saintlike passion"; and the experience created an image of unchanging purity.

The consequence of that experience, however, is not the fixing of innocence, the embodiment of the mythical within their own experience as Ibsen had projected it before, but on the contrary, the descent of both of them into a life of actual sexuality—within the metaphor of the play, a movement from light into darkness. For Irene, her life after this "episode" is a life beyond the grave: "I went into the darkness—when the child stood transfigured in the light. . . . I have stood on the turntable in variety shows. Posed as a naked statue in living pictures. I have earned a great deal of money." And Irene describes killing her children, one after another, as they are born. In the ways in which this dramatic poem works to define the content of *child* and *childhood*, the repeated insistence upon killing the child of the statue and the killing of her other "children" seems to identify the purging of that which *child* represents within her life—the killing of innocence and the movement into the world of experience. That their "child" is dead within their imagination is clarified in Rubek's recollection that Irene conceived of museums as "grave vaults." There is also a tension between Irene's conception of the image, formed out of *living* clay, and Rubek's final version of the statue completed in *cold* marble, fixed and unchanging and—within Irene's imagination— dead. Rubek's modification of the statue is also a form of killing their child, and it signals his movement from innocence into sexual experience. That condition is seen as a kind of death—although it might be more accurate to say that the deathlike quality of existence comes after these characters have been wasted and disillusioned by their sexual experience. In any case, their desire is for a resurrection, an awakening into a new childhood.

One of the most crucial concepts within *When We Dead Awaken* is that held in the metaphor of awakening. Initially, awakening is seen as a kind of resurrection. The metaphor of the statue is the first use of this image. Here the young girl awakens, transfigured, having transcended human life, moving into a new and purified experience. Irene sees herself as awakening from a kind of death. Her death is her sensual life after she left Rubek; and her awakening is actually a movement from phenomenally oriented experience to the development of a mythical experience which ends in death. Both Irene and Rubek—in their metaphoric death—have lived within the abyss (to use Ibsen's own imagery). Rubek's art has changed from an idealization of experience (from poetry in Irene's terms) to a satiric ridicule of human beings which is a recognition of an implicit bestiality in the people whose portraits he models. His recent or post-Irene work is a realistic confrontation with human experience, the antithesis of art as he conceived it earlier.

Rubek and Irene see the ascent of the mountain as a form of awakening, a resurrection. The most important thing to consider in *When We Dead Awaken* is the quality of the ascent. This final movement in the play is first suggested as Maja reminds Rubek that he once promised her that he would take her up upon a high mountain and show her "all the glory of the world." Rubek inadvertently suggests in his response to her that this was a promise which he had made to someone else, and later it is clear that the vow was initially made to Irene. However, in this initial discussion of the promise, Rubek says:

> That is a sort of saying which I was in the habit of using for a time. . . . Yes, something from school days. The sort of thing to lure the neighbors' children

with when I wanted them to come out and play with
me in the woods and on the mountains.

To lure a child out to play in several ways does describe
Rubek's imaginative response to his relationship with
both Irene and Maja. In the final act, the roles are re-
versed. Irene lures Rubek: "you should rather go up
high into the mountains. As high as ever you can. Higher,
higher—always higher, Arnold." There is the usual paradigm in this work of height and light; to this is added
the additional resonances of awakening and childhood.
The image of the awakening child is a metaphor of a
sexual object which does not threaten with guilt. However, it is impossible to ignore the associations with the
sense of death which this image contains. The movement
into light, as these characters sense it, is a movement
away from life, from an actual life into a mythical or
illusory existence.

The energy which once would have caused Rubek to
lose his self-identification in sexual experience in a submission to instinct now causes him to give up phenomenal experience in a willed renunciation of life which
takes the form of a fantasy of sexuality. The relationship
of Rubek and Irene never exists outside of fantasy: in
the creative play of the creation of "The Resurrection
Day" which is play in the sense that it enacts a relationship which is not realized in actual experience; in the
little games on the shores of the Lake of Taunitz and the
brook, and the final and serious play at the resolution of
the action in which the two act out a marriage ceremony
in climbing the mountain.

The scene in the second act, in which Rubek and
Irene reenact their game of floating leaves upon the Lake
of Taunitz, seems particularly significant in presenting
the quality of their relationship. The primary quality of
this action is, of course, its play; it is the acting out of a
dream of freedom in which the leaves and flowers become birds and boats, floating out into the freedom of
the sea.

It is important to remember that this scene is a re-enactment of their past—a game played during the time of the creation of the statue. The primary revelation here is the quality of their evasion of reality. It is another example of Ibsen's use of the image of the sea as the illusion of freedom, but the sense of the sea in this play is attenuated in the re-creation of the game of sailing "boats" upon the Lake of Taunitz. However, the quality of this image of the sea is crucial. Insistently throughout the plays Ibsen uses the sea as a displacement of the abyss, a metaphor of the illusion of freedom and the underlying reality of death. *When We Dead Awaken* is no exception. Ulfheim, the hunter who lures Maja into the forests in search of direct experience, is associated with the sea; he describes the waters of Rubek's projected coastal voyage as "sickly gutters," announcing that he arrived not by steamer but by sailing his own cutter. But in the relationship between Rubek and Irene the desire for freedom and the realization of desire is weakened to the point that there is only the game of setting out to sea—actually, only the re-creation of a game previously played. The game shares its strategy with the creative work of the statue. Its purpose is to act out the relationship within a form which preserves its innocence. The game moves the relationship back into childhood. Certainly it is significant that this game is reenacted in the place where the actual children were playing just moments before. Ibsen's use of children in this scene is extremely revealing. The initial scene of the second act in which Rubek and Maja formulate their estrangement is played in counterpoint to the play of the real children:

> . . . *in the distance, on the high plateau, on the other side of the brook, a troop of singing children is playing and dancing. Some are wearing city clothes, some in rural costume. Their happy laughter is heard, softened during the following.*

When Irene comes, she is surrounded by the children. She sends them off, and takes her place beside the brook, letting "the stream of water flow over her hands, cooling them." She assumes, unmistakenly, Rubek's pose in the modified sculpture in his gesture of expiation. At the conclusion of the little game, Rubek asks Irene to join him at the villa at Lake Taunitz, built on the sight of their earlier play. He asks her to unlock the casket of his creativity, using the devious metaphor he used before to hide the meaning of his relationship with Irene from Maja. She refuses.

IRENE.   Empty dreams! Futile dead dreams. *Our* life together has no resurrection.
RUBEK (*curtly, breaking off*).   Then let us continue to play.
IRENE.   Yes, playing—only playing!
(*They sit and strew leaves and petals out in the brook and let them float and sail away.*)

It is from this condition that they build their dream of climbing the mountain to their marriage. From one perspective the ascent is a denial of the form, the restraint, the static nature of art in an attempt to realize life, building upon their recognition that they have never lived. In this interpretation it is the antithesis of Rubek's earlier choice which affirmed the task and denied the sexual. However, it is also seen in the terms of the play as the antithesis of the descent into sexuality of Maja and Ulfheim. Ulfheim's profession is also presented as a battle with death, but in his case, that confrontation does not exist in the creation of an illusion but in experience itself. His sexuality is obvious, seen in association with images of bestiality. His virile ugliness tempts Maja, and she declares that there is nothing of the artist in him. There is, however, even in her experience, the pattern of expectation and disillusionment. Ulfheim promises to take her to his castle in the mountains, but when they arrive it is a filthy hut and Ulfheim's promise is seen as a clear strategy to seduce Maja. However, her recognition of the situation includes an implicit acceptance of her own situation, and, after meeting Irene and Rubek, they make the choice to descend the mountain, avoiding the danger of the storm. Their action of descent helps to define the action of the artist and model. Rubek and Irene, as dead awakened, are in the fixed state of innocence which is the condition of the naked girl of the statue: the "resurrection" suggests an awakening to an unsensual love. And yet that state is as destructive in its second realization as it is in its first: their ascent is met with the avalanche and they both are killed.

The relationship between the image of the statue, the child of Irene and Rubek, and the action of the drama is clear and yet difficult. The central action of the play, the reunion of Irene and Rubek, is the resurrection of Irene. In her own imagination, it is a resurrection because of her *death*, the loss of her soul to Rubek. In one sense, the figure of Rubek himself in the revised grouping of the famous statue is an image of his expiation; and his confrontation with the guilt he bears in his contribution to Irene's death is matched in the action of *When We Dead Awaken*. The statue, as well, represents an unnatural fixing of a state in time; the relationship of Irene and Rubek is also fixed in the moment of their mutual death. The similarity of that death to the death of Brand and Gerd is certainly not accidental. Both deaths are the immediate answer to a renunciation of sexuality, the denial of that aspect of the self which would find realization in the union of the self with another human being.

Rubek feels that he has found Irene and can elect life once again, that he has opportunity once more, but Irene denies the possibility of such a second chance:

IRENE. . . . The desire for life died within me, Arnold. Now I am resurrected. And I search for you. And find you. And then I see that you and life are dead, as I have been.

PROFESSOR RUBEK. How wrong you are! Life within us and around us ferments and surges as before.

IRENE (*smiling and shaking her head*). Your young

resurrected girl can see the whole of life lying dead.

PROFESSOR RUBEK (*throwing his arms violently around her*).   Then let us two dead beings live life once to the fullest before we go down into our graves again!

IRENE (*with a scream*).   Arnold!

PROFESSOR RUBEK.   But not here in the half-darkness! Not here where the ugly, wet burial linen enshrouds us—

IRENE (*enthralled with passion*).   No, no—up in the light and all in the glittering splendor. Up to the summit of promise!

PROFESSOR RUBEK.   Up there we will perform our wedding celebration, Irene—my beloved!

IRENE (*proudly*).   The sun may look upon us, Arnold.

PROFESSOR RUBEK.   All the powers of light may look upon us. And those of darkness as well. (*grips her hand*) Will you follow me, my bride of grace?

IRENE (*as though transfigured*).   I follow you, willingly and happily, my lord and master.

PROFESSOR RUBEK (*drawing her toward him*).   We must first go through the mist, Irene, and then—

IRENE.   Yes, through all the mists. And then straight up to the tower's summit which shines in the sunrise.

This assertion is analogous to the paradoxical ascent of Solness in *The Master Builder*. Ulfheim has clarified the danger of their climb and the difficulty of their situation. It would be dangerous enough merely to stay at the place they are; but they go forward toward the storm which is descending the mountain, through the mists (which as Ulfheim notes will shroud them like winding sheets). Their action is the suicidal course of Rebekka and Rosmer; it is an imitation passion, an imaginary marriage which is, in reality, a suicide. The paradoxical nature of the choice is implicit in its metaphors. The metaphor of the abyss is clearly present with its relationship to the terrifying and comforting image of the sea, the sense of a mythical freedom which is, in reality, a confrontation with the self, and the sense of the final triumph, the achievement of light which is freedom, self-assertion, blessing, sanctity, innocence, will achieved, and sensuality encompassed.

The desire of Ibsen's hero is to achieve innocence and pleasure; and the imitation marriage does attempt that impossibility, but maintains or achieves innocence through making the actual pleasure an impossibility. Rubek destroys the threat which Irene poses for him just as Rosmer sacrifices the dangerous Rebekka. The black-dressed sister of mercy appears at the conclusion of the play, obviously searching for Irene, witnesses her death in the avalanche, and offers a final blessing—suggesting a triumph of asceticism. Her presence at this moment, black against the white of the snow, an image of restriction acutely visual against the sound of Maja's song of freedom, is certainly a deliberately strong theatrical gesture. The imagery of darkness and light is compressed in Ibsen's use of this pair of figures: the image of Irene, dressed in white, and the sister of mercy, dressed in black. The sister is obviously an image of confinement, even punishment. On the literal level of the play she is a kind of keeper for the apparently mentally damaged Irene. She has with her a straitjacket kept to restrain her patient if she gets violent, according to Irene's report. This suggestion relates the sister to that image of death-within-life which Irene develops, her description of being forcibly lowered into a padded room with her arms held behind her.

One aspect of the resolution of this play is certainly the sense of the final act as an expiation. It is a mutual sacrifice made, as Solness's sacrifice is made, to atone for past crimes. However, the sense of expiation here is very complex: Irene and Rubek condemn themselves for a crime against themselves, for denying the vitality of their sexual relationship and "killing" themselves. Their awakening, in one sense, is an awakening to their guilt. Irene, for example, experiences some sense of release when Rubek admits his guilt: "You have a shadow that tortures me. And I have my oppressive conscience." His recognition of his own guilt is necessary for the reformation of their relationship which is to be their mutual sacrifice and expiation. The sense of their death-in-life, the period of darkness in which both abandoned themselves to sensual experience, is also present as an image of guilt. Irene's shadow, of course, is that sister of mercy; and while her necessity clarifies Rubek's crime against Irene (in that he is responsible for the quality of her life), there is also some sense of Irene's own guilt for her behavior. Her own identification with the figure of the statue clarifies her desire to awaken in innocence.

The nature of the sacrifice which insures that Irene and Rubek will maintain an innocent, asexual relationship is also related to the action as an expiation. Their sacrifice purifies them, removing the possibility of a relationship which would bring them guilt at the same time it offers them the satisfaction of punishing themselves for denying that relationship. Rubek and Irene make the ascent into a known danger; they see clearly that their movement is toward death. However, they disguise that movement in a rhetoric which presents the illusion of that act as a choice of life. They are then destroyed, as Brand is destroyed, by the release of energy which has been restrained. They choose an actual death, phrased within an imagery of life, after having lived within an existence they disguised with an imagery of death.

The quality of Ibsen's resolution of *When We Dead Awaken* is typically paradoxical, and that paradox contains a strong and undisguised despair. Maja's song of freedom frames the destructive avalanche; it is heard both before and after the vision of Irene and Rubek destroyed:

> *I am free! I am free! I am free!*
> *My captive life is past!*
> *I am free as a bird! I am free!*

This play contains an unelaborated but important tension between a sense of being frozen, fixed and static within stone or ice, or flexible, malleable (capable of being modeled, changed, and worked upon). This opposition is clear in the contrast in Irene's imagination between the *living* clay in which the sculptor's image is created and the *dead* marble in which it is finished. The sense of being restricted, put into a grave, a cold and damp room, or a windowless and gilded chamber; lowered into a padded vault, or being caught and held within the stone of a sculptured portrait is opposed to the sense of being freed from imprisoning rooms, of moving into clear and unfettered space from which the whole world can be seen. In the metaphoric opposition of height and depth, there is the distinction between the dense forests in which Ulfheim hunts and the clear, if barren, mountains to which Rubek and Irene attempt to climb. Each objective offers the temptation of freedom. The consequence of Rubek's freedom is, of course, being imprisoned within the crushing force of the avalanche. The antithetical freedom voiced by Maja is not the freedom of realizing one's will; it is not the freedom of experience as the manifestation of conscious intention. The freedom of *When We Dead Awaken* is the freedom of being able to be part of a natural process, of mutability and change. In many ways it is a vision of experience as destructive, hostile, giving and taking. That freedom is best illustrated in Ulfheim's image; and he, too, is presented as a victim. His objective of affection and love has also been taken from him. The reality in *When We Dead Awaken* is loss and substitution, and the movement into illusion is an attempt to escape that recognition. The final moments of Ibsen's last play present this movement more clearly than in the preceding plays. *When We Dead Awaken* discloses Ibsen's sense of the failure of mythical thinking, the failure of any scheme which gives the self a sense of integral identity and continuity and successful will. However, the play also clarifies that Ibsen saw the self as unable to deal with phenomenal experience without myth. The paradox of Ibsen builds upon his recognition of the failure and the necessity of mythological thinking.

8

Recapitulation

The essential unity of Ibsen's work is obvious. The same general actions occur again and again from *Brand* to *When We Dead Awaken,* and the repetition of the central metaphors is insistent. However, the general dramatic structures which hold the basic drama are very different. Even within the three expansive dramas, *Brand, Peer Gynt,* and *Emperor and Galilean,* Ibsen seems to make a conscious effort toward projecting a greater sense of realism. In *Emperor and Galilean* he abandons verse for prose with the deliberate aim of creating a more plausible and realistic work. The influences working upon Ibsen which would lead him into a more realistic form are complex, but certain major pressures are obvious. The insistence in the late nineteenth century upon phenomenal cause, the interest in the relationship between environment and character, the increasing emphasis upon the concept of the universe as man-centered and not God-centered certainly focused the work of literature upon man and the specific environment which contained his experience and which participated in determining it. One of the features which marks the difference between Ibsen's earlier, more expansive dramas and the more controlled and focused plays of the period of *A Doll's House* through *Rosmersholm* is a greater attention to the human and natural environment in which his basic drama takes place.

The pressure to respond to his own keen sense of the malicious self-interest in his contemporary society is clear even in *Brand*. The characterization of such figures as the Dean and the Mayor in this play shows that Ibsen's attention was directed at least partially toward exposing the hypocrisies, the exploitations, and the apathies which offended him in his own experience. That satiric voice answers a demand within Ibsen for topical revelance. However, the major function of these characters, indeed all the characters in *Brand*, is to define what the Brand consciousness is. Their energy is directed toward their own self-interest, and they consistently sacrifice the integrity of their individual vocations to provide themselves more comfort, sensual pleasure, and reputation. Actually, we know little else about them; they exist merely to provide the antithesis of Brand's concept of an integral, self-determining will—a will which is also self-directed, but self-directed in order to become committed to an absolute, not for immediate phenomenal satisfaction.

In *Brand, Peer Gynt,* and *Emperor and Galilean* the relationship between the protagonist and the other characters is more expressionistic than realistic; that is, the characters are clarifications of the movements within the hero's own consciousness. In these plays Ibsen presents a hero who is confronted with a series of characters who are embodiments of choices which he must make. The dramas proceed in a series of episodes which test the integrity of the hero. However, the dialectic between good and evil is not absolute; the hero is in a state of anxiety because the relationship between good and evil seems to shift. The transforming images of Agnes, The Woman in Green, Helena, and Makrina are examples of that flux. Each, for a particular moment, embodies a value for the hero toward which he moves; then each is transformed into a source of restriction, pain, and guilt. These figures serve the single purpose of revealing the way in which the hero's consciousness operates, and the only development or complexity which they have as characters derives from the fact that the hero's image of them changes. They are projections of an ambivalence in the consciousness of the hero.

In the development of the more realistic plays, the primary experience of the hero stays the same, but the way in which his experience is projected through the peripheral or functional characters is extremely different. For example: both Brand and Rosmer attempt to free themselves from a guilt which they see as a familial inheritance; both of them see the conventional Christian church as hypocritical and voice their own desire for innocence in a mission in which they are the agent of a universal emancipation and ennoblement; both of them are tempted by sexuality, and both deny their wives, seeing sexuality as a restriction of their vocation; both of them become disillusioned; and both die in a suicidal act (although Brand's ascent to the known danger of the Ice Church is less deliberately suicidal). Each, as well, dies with a female figure who functions in some way as an image of his own guilt. And yet, the similarity between the temperaments of Brand and Rosmer is minimal. Brand is aggressive, dominating, and cruel in his indifference to the suffering of others, and Rosmer is passive, gentle, and ineffective. However, in Ibsen's exploration of the limits of power which the self holds, the emphasis clearly shifts from *Brand* to *Rosmersholm*. Brand's idealism is not the manifestation of his ability to declare himself free from the temptations of phenomenal experience but, on the contrary, is an unconscious evasion of such experience; his movement toward the Ice Church is not a positive act but an escape from all which is represented by the abyss. The sense of the movement as an escape is subtle, however, and perhaps, not even a part of Ibsen's own conscious scheme. In *Rosmersholm* the superficial pose of heroism is deliberately abandoned; there is no sense of the consciousness being free. Rosmer is clearly the victim of conflicting pressures—the demands of sexuality and the need to see the self free from those demands in an ordered vision of reality which would halt the processes of experience. The sacrifice which Brand's concept of identity demands is painful for him, but he sees that pain as part of his identity as he enacts a ritual of martyrdom which would allow him to transcend the phenomenal reality of his experience. However, the complexity of reality comes down upon him, literally and figuratively, in the Ice Church; and he is forced to confront the fact that the tension between the mythical and the phenomenal is not a simple dialectic in which it is possible to affirm the one and deny the other. Rosmer is less an aggressive and confident hero, less a hero in the conventional sense, because the reality in which he moves is more clearly complex, equivocal, and confusing.

The threatening complexity of that reality is presented by Ibsen primarily in the greater density of the characters which define the conflict for the hero. Agnes has a minimal inner life; Rebekka has a past and a present, an external and inner experience as complex as Rosmer's. However, she is not a co-hero as some critics suggest. She has a complex reality which is disclosed to Rosmer; and that disclosure is the primary event in his experience. Rebekka is for Rosmer what Agnes is for Brand—the object of his lust. That object undergoes a transformation as it moves from an image of innocence to an image of guilt, a confirmation of the sexuality (and the incompleteness, irrationality, and mortality) of the hero. However, as an aspect of the total consciousness represented by the play, Rebekka does far more than Agnes. In the more simple structure of *Brand*, Agnes changes as an image within Brand's consciousness. In *Rosmersholm*, the disclosure of Rebekka's character is an actual event which occurs to Rosmer, to us, and—to an interesting degree—to Rebekka herself. Her recognition of the truth of her identity, which comes to her through Kroll, is a realization that she is guilty of incest and that she, too, has inherited a guilt which finds its source in her family. Rebekka is not merely a projection of Rosmer's movement from the hope of innocence to disillusionment; she is an individual entity within the play who suffers an analogous experience and can, therefore, function more complexly as the principal object with which his consciousness deals. Rebekka then be-

comes not merely the illusion of innocence being transformed into guilt but an embodiment of the process. The
secondary characters in these plays are not merely aspects of the protagonist's consciousness but are themselves processes of consciousness.

Hedvig's suicide signals an event within Hjalmar's
psyche in a death which is somewhat analogous to the
death of Alf in *Brand*. Alf's death is clearly the manifestation of Brand's renunciation. Alf is the temptation to
attach himself to a human relationship which would diffuse his will. He is also the embodiment of guilt which
needs to be sacrificed in order to expiate that guilt. His
death is an event which happens to Brand and to Agnes
—principally to Brand, although Agnes's renunciation
anticipates and parallels her husband's. Hedvig's death
also happens to her. It fulfills the same function as Alf's
death as an event in the hero's consciousness. It is a confirmation of Hjalmar's failure, the destruction of that
which affirms his identity; it is the answer to his own renunciation of Hedvig and, at the same time, the proof of
her love. The sacrifice of the actual Hedvig allows him
to preserve the illusion of her, an illusion which could
not have been maintained in reality. However, Hedvig's
action is also her own movement from a damaged and
painful reality into an illusion; it is the extremity of the
commitment to an aggressive, illusionary, and mythical
vision of reality.

The demand of realism is to create a body of characters whose behavior is plausible in terms of acceptable
notions of what people will do in given circumstances.
The given circumstances must include an environment
which is described in detail and appears to be related to
those places which we ourselves experience. Primarily,
however, the processes of action must give the illusion of
being determined by the particular relationships of the
characters. That is, there must be a clear and conceivable
chain of events seen in a cause and effect sequence.
Working on the basis of the Scribean *pièce-bien-faite*,
Ibsen contained his essential drama within a sequence of

events, interlocking and complex, but clearly evident. The apparent or external cause of the action in Ibsen's realistic plays is the accidental meeting at a particular point in time of a series of individual movements which are related but at the same time independent. Without the coincidence of family, school, and social revolt against Kroll's authority, he would not have intruded into the world of Rosmer and Rebekka and initiated the series of revelations and private disclosures that intrusion caused in *Rosmersholm*. If Hedda's return had not coincided with Eilert's reentry into society and if Tessman had not found the manuscript and so on, that particular action would not have resolved in the same way in *Hedda Gabler*.

However, any awareness of Ibsen's central drama makes it possible to see that the events and their peculiar resolution are inevitable within Ibsen's vision of consciousness. The creation of a project which puts experience, past, present, and future into some kind of comprehensible form—Eilert's history of mankind—is only an illusion of reality, not an understanding of reality itself, and that illusion is vulnerable to phenomenal experience and is destroyed by it. The only means of gaining a sense of form which is free from dissolution or change is to create some sense of form out of death. The suicides of Hedvig, Rosmer, Rebekka, Eilert, and Hedda are inevitable as the manifestation of a particular strategy of consciousness; to fix the self within a comprehensible vision of reality is to remove the self from the flux of phenomenal experience—to die and escape consciousness and the phenomena which feed it. These deaths are the consequence of that basic premise. However, the demands of the realistic form make it necessary for Ibsen to give those actions a plausibility within the specifically realistic world of the play.

Fulfilling the demand of realism to create more plausible, individually motivated characters, Ibsen worked to give more density to the imaginations of those characters in strong relation to his hero. I have already discussed the ways in which that character who provides an erotic object for the hero is developed with greater complexity in *Rosmersholm* than in *Brand,* but the increased sense of characterization in the realistic works accomplishes even more than that extra resonance. In the more realistic plays, Ibsen created worlds in which a series of characters enacted the basic drama, each in his individual experience. For example, in *The Wild Duck,* Hjalmar suffers the loss of his illusory vision of reality, a loss which the exposure and death of his "child" Hedvig embodies. However, the falsity of his image of Hjalmar is exposed to Gregers and functions as a dissolving illusion; Hjalmar's sudden renunciation of Hedvig destroys her created image of him which she seeks to regain. In *Rosmersholm,* both Rebekka and Rosmer function as images of illusion for each other; Rosmer suffers the transformation of the concept of the innocent Rebekka, and Rebekka is unable to accommodate the movement of Rosmer from innocent into erotic and makes her own renunciation. The primary focus remains on the consciousness of Rosmer, but a paradigmatic structure is also at work. In *The Master Builder,* Hilde is Solness's object of tempting innocence seen simultaneously as a bird of prey hunting him down. Their final relationship is a focused ambivalence: he fulfills her demand and falls; she inspires and kills. But each functions for the other. In *When We Dead Awaken,* the antithesis of the mythical and the phenomenal is very clear; and the movement toward the mythical voices itself in the desire for innocence, the desire to awake into some kind of transformed experience. Both Rubek and Irene seek each other as objects of desire, and yet they function for each other as embodiments of guilt. The ambivalent movement in the consciousness of each is to seek and destroy the object of love, and the resolution contains that ambiguity as they lead each other to their death in the form of marriage.

In his more realistic plays Ibsen compressed the metaphoric structure of his private vision within a concentrated and highly formal structure. This structure has been considered classic in its unwavering focus and clear movement. The more open forms in which he worked—the dramatic-epic poem of *Brand,* the psuedo-folk drama of *Peer Gynt,* the history play of *Emperor and Galilean* —certainly had a set of conventions in which Ibsen moved. The conventions of these more open and episodic forms, however, are less restrictive. Consequently, the basic drama is able to range more freely among its images and lacks the intensification which that drama achieved when it was compressed into a more controlled structure.

One of the conventions of realistic literature is the closely developed representation of environment. Realism is one of the responses to the scientific conception of the environment as a determinant of experience, and in drama that emphasis was answered in an increased attention to the scene. This attention resulted both in a structural emphasis upon conditions determining character and a more natural physical environment in the stage setting itself. In Ibsen's case one of the results of his exploration of realism is his exclusive use of naturalistic interiors from *Pillars of Society* to *The Master Builder.*

The contained space of the rooms in which Ibsen's realistic dramas take place becomes a limited area in which each major object assumes importance—these rooms and the figures they hold become the phenomenal field in which the basic drama of consciousness voices itself. The spatial metaphor which is a kind of metaphysical landscape is displaced into the rooms, objects, and imaginative conceptions of those who inhabit them. The process of displacing this basic metaphoric structure is one of concealing its content in order to make its presence plausible. The process of transporting the image of the sea into the realistic environment of *The Wild Duck* demonstrates how that displacement adds layers of meaning and resonance to the basic metaphor. In the first place, Ibsen's use of the images of the sea and the forest are related—the darkness and density of the forest,

the sense of it as wilderness, is close to his imaginative
concept of the sea as dark, uncontrollable energy, irrationality. Also, both the sea and the forest are associated with a sense of primitive eroticism in his imagination, as we have seen. In *The Wild Duck*, these
images meet in the strangeness of the created forest in
the garret, that place which Hedvig sees as "the bottom
of the sea." The place is a sanctuary for the Ekdals
which is obviously analogous to the mythical heights
which Brand and Julian use as sanctuary, but here that
movement is seen as the consequence of damaging experience working upon powerless men. The garret is an
escape from the threats and demands of reality. Most
significantly it is a created place, a synthetic environment
which attempts to re-create the past. The density of
Ibsen's characterization of Hedvig allows him to use her
childlike fantasy to identify the place as "the bottom of
the sea," seeing the garret as being like the tangled
weeds growing on the bottom of the sea floor which held
the real wild duck when it dove down to the bottom of
the sea. The place is, then, related to death—the objective
of the duck's suicidal dive. The withered trees, the rabbits and doves which substitute for the wild and free
bears and eagles, the images of death and the hourglass
in the book of engravings, references to the world of the
Flying Dutchman—all work together to project a concept of this created environment, which is the mythical
strategy of this play, as regressive, illusory, synthetic,
restrictive, and self-destructive. The metaphor moves
from its original promise as a place of comfort and protection into the threatening, self-destructive place of
Hedvig's suicide. Also, this creation of an artificial place,
a personally constructed forest and sea, shows more
clearly than ever before in Ibsen's plays that the act of
creating and using a myth is an attempt to encompass
the phenomenal without being subject to it. The substance of the garret is the material which is an unthreatening substitute for phenomena seen as dangerous. The
compression and concentration of the concealed images

of the forest and the sea as they meet in the garret reveals the complexity of their content much more fully than in the less developed use of them earlier.

The Ekdal's use of this created place illustrates a basic method in Ibsen's use of metaphor. The scenic detail of the garret is not a projection of the hero's consciousness in any simple sense. It is not the relatively unambiguous transformation of the tree into the skeleton of Kaiser's expressionistic *From Morn to Midnight*. The complexity of the garret as a metaphor comes from the fact that it is not the projection of a state of consciousness but rather a process of consciousness. The metaphoric structure is the field of consciousness itself as it gropes for an understanding of its own function, exploring these images to see what they can do to provide a sense of form which can contain the processes of thought. The distinction between seeing these metaphors as projections of process rather than embodiments of condition may be small, but it is extremely significant in an understanding of Ibsen's use of verbal and visual imagery. This distinction explains why fixed interpretations of Ibsen's metaphoric structure are not satisfying.

The rhetorical process in which the basic images transform themselves into their opposites also explains the basic ambiguity in Ibsen's use of realism. If Ibsen's middle plays are to be seen as realistic, they must be interpreted as representations of an actual social and natural environment. Ibsen, of course, represented reality as unattainable in the shifting processes of mythical and phenomenological thinking. But he did work within a form which pretended and, perhaps, intended to be realistic; and it is necessary to think more about that ambiguous choice of form. As a base, I would like to begin with the definition of realism which I find most satisfactory, Georg Lukács statement from *Studies in European Realism*:

> The central category and criterion of realist literature is the type, a particular synthesis which organ-

ically binds together the general and particular both in characters and situations. What makes a type a type is not its average quality, not its mere individual being, however profoundly conceived; what makes it a type is that in it all the humanly and socially essential determinants are present on their highest level of development, in the ultimate unfolding of the possibilities latent in them, in extreme presentation of their extremes, rendering concrete the peaks and limits of men and epochs.

True great realism thus depicts man and society as complete entities, instead of showing merely one or the other of their aspects. Measured by this criterion, artistic trends determined by either exclusive introspection or exclusive extraversion equally impoverish and distort reality. Thus realism means a three-dimensionality, an all-roundness, that endows with independent life characters and human relationships. It by no means involves a rejection of the emotional and intellectual dynamism which necessarily develops together with the modern world. All it opposes is the destruction of the completeness of the human personality and of the objective typicality of men and situations through an excessive cult of the momentary mood. The struggle against such tendencies acquired a decisive importance in the realist literature of the nineteenth century.[1]

Lukács finds realism coming into focus at moments of social transition and sees the realist writer as a participant in the processes of change. He defines the objective of realism as the objective of literature, "the concept of the complete human personality as the social and historical task humanity has to solve."[2] Lukács himself sees the tension in Ibsen's drama between the perfection of its form, which he affirms as classic, and a disturbing depiction of reality: "imperfectly its formal perception concealed the inner instability of Ibsen's conception of society and hence of his real dramatic form." [3] Lukács does not develop this concept of Ibsen's instable vision of society and consequent instable dramatic form; but his response is predictable. As a Marxist critic of realism, Lukács sees society as capable of resolution: the writer is a participant in a progressive movement. Ibsen's drama is, on the surface, critical of society; and the figures of the Dean and the Major in *Brand*, Manders in *Ghosts*, even Kroll in *Rosmersholm*, seem to be personifications of what Ibsen saw as evil and exploitative in society. In one sense, the ethics which these figures voice do provide the restrictions and oppressions which Ibsen's heroes face and attempt to transcend. However, these figures are only pale reflections of the real restriction and oppression experienced by Ibsen's heroes. The demand to renounce sensual pleasure and freedom—which is, surely, the primary ethical restriction voiced by these hypocrites—is much more strongly present within the consciousness of the hero himself. Brand's renunciation of Agnes and Alf, Rosmer's denial of both Beate and Rebekka, Solness's movement away from eroticism into fantasy—all these acts of denial are motivated by internal, not social, demands which voice personal guilt. It would be possible, of course, to argue that the presence of guilt is, indeed, the embodiment in consciousness of the values of the particular society which Ibsen attacks. His insistence that the son inherits his parent's guilt suggests the Freudian concept of the superego as the manifestation of a social or familial restriction within the individual psyche. Certainly this concept is operative in the plays, but guilt in these plays is also something more than the Freudian superego asserting itself. Sexual processes are metaphors for the consciousness of phenomenal experience. Sexuality is the most acute phenomenal experience; within sexual experience *process*—gain and loss, value and distaste, desire and satisfaction, completion and dependence,—is all exposed to us. Guilt in Ibsen's drama concentrates in fear of phenomenal experience, fear and rejection. Guilt is a protection from the pain of losing a sense of identity in the flux of phenomenal events; and the impetus to be free of guilt is the energy which develops the individual myth. Ibsen's conception of society is a displacement of his conception of the consciousness. This, perhaps, is why Lukács is disturbed by it. Ibsen's vision of reality is a vision of consciousness and is undeniably pessimistic. The oppressions and restrictions are intrinsic and irredeemable. The final focus in each of Ibsen's major plays is upon a dissolving sense of reality, and the resolution of these plays insists that there is no way to create order outside of the fragile structures of consciousness. Ibsen is guilty of the subjectivism which Lukács decries despite the fact that his apparently realistic forms disguise that intense and "exclusive introspection."

Lukács discusses the formal integrity of Ibsen's dramas as cohesive and efficient in form, producing a classic structure which almost conceals the "inner instability" of his perception of reality. Of course, Lukács interprets this ambiguity as a weakness since that inconsistency undermines the realistic base of the plays. I would argue, of course, from the opposite point of view, seeing the tension created between Ibsen's formal realism and his conceptual subjectivity as a strength. Our age would judge that realism is no longer a sufficiently open dramatic form because it assumes a simplistic approach to experience which is inconsistent with our recognition of the complexity and subjectivity of our response to human experience. In the detail and temporal flexibility of the novel it is more possible to encompass a greater sense of that complexity within a more or less realistic frame. A novel can assume the voice of an introspective consciousness directly, but the conventions of drama present a figure objectively: he is seen and heard as an external object in relationship to the other figures in some environment which is external to the spectator. The process of identification in which the self of the spectator relates to the emotional movements of the play as if they were his own experience breaks down that objectivity. But the imaginative event begins with the spectator seeing and hearing the actors as objects apart from him; and, on one level of consciousness, at least, they remain detached and objective. The experience of identification in which the spectator responds to analogies between his own personal psychic movements and the strategies of consciousness within the play is not based upon a one-to-one relationship between him and the hero. Ibsen begins with an objective realism; and as the play develops and movements of emotional energy are generated, the spectator's identification is distributed among these movements. For example, in *Rosmersholm* the strong desire for a satisfying, integrated relationship with another human being which is free both of guilt and a fear of loss is brought into focus by the characterization of both Rosmer and Rebekka. The spectator identifies not so much with the specific character but with the emotional reality of that desire. The condemnation of that desire as the source of self-destruction and the violation of innocence voices itself clearly in the play as well, and the spectator's repulsion at Rebekka's cunning scheme to destroy Beate is a process of identification with the fear of irrationality and the desire for control which manifests itself in the acts of renunciation made by Rosmer and Rebekka. Also, the deliberately obscure metaphor of the white horses provides a focal point. His conscious imagination denies the reality of such supernatural creatures, laughing with Rebekka at Madam Hespeth. However, the content of the metaphor—the fascination with unknown energy and the equally strong dread of seeing still present that which has been destroyed or overcome—does have reality for him; and the gradual revelation of the substance of that image to both Rosmer and Rebekka is experienced by the spectator as a personal disclosure.

The objective reality of Ibsen's plays seems to present an understandable reality as the plays begin, but the work of these plays destroys that objective comprehension even within the strict formalism of his organized structure. In the works of Beckett, Ionesco, Genet, and Arrabal the poet's personal recognition of the obscurity of experience has produced plays which defy conventional temporal sequence and break down the conventions of character and plot. It is important to realize, however, that Ibsen also works to abrogate those concepts even within the taut structure of his realistic plays. The realism of those plays from A Doll's House to Rosmersholm is, in itself, a dramatic metaphor. Ibsen seems to say: Reality might appear to take the form which I imitate here, and yet that form is merely a tentative construct of our imagination which allows us to explore the processes in which our imaginations are able to create and respond to certain self-conscious experiences; we must begin with this formal structure because it is necessary to isolate and organize events within some sense of temporal sequence in order to conceptualize experience. Invariably in Ibsen's realistic plays the action is the exposure of the past. Essentially, however, that exposure only takes the form of disclosures of the past; the real revelation is of the quality of the present, and the action is the surfacing of information about the self which had been hidden or disguised in some way. The exposure always isolates the tension between the mythical and the phenomenal. The exposure also reveals the falsity of his personal myth in such a way that the hero cannot partake of the phenomenal experience he desires. The past is not the past in any simple sense in these plays; it is the exposed present: the real identity of Hedvig, the present diseased Alving, the sexuality of Rosmer and Rebekka, the dead Rubek and Irene. The resolution of these plays is the disintegration of the realistic base on which they proceed. Ibsen's drama exposes the invalidity of the external projection of order and reveals the subjective consciousness as the only reality.

The object which we identify as the play, whether it

be the text which we read in private or the performance we experience publicly, is the complex stimulus which works upon us to produce the response which is our conception of the play. The complexity and thoroughness of our response depends upon the complexity and thoroughness of the stimuli. I have discussed seven of Ibsen's plays as organizations of images which take us through explorations of certain strategies of consciousness. The structural organization of realism is the method in which Ibsen was most successful in conducting these explorations. We have laid aside, I trust, that attitude which would evaluate these plays on the basis of their closeness to our conception of the phenomena of nature and human behavior. The re-creation of a surface which appeared to be realistic in that sense is Ibsen's medium; the confrontation with the existence of certain processes of consciousness is the significant reality of these plays. The particular density of language and visual image in Ibsen's realistic plays is the result of his exploration of the ambiguous and often obscure workings of consciousness which we have been discussing. This dramatic form provided a structure in which those explorations could take place and voice themselves in such a way that they would stimulate our response. In Strindberg's nonrealistic plays, the playwright attempted to free his spectators from the restrictions of conventional response by using obviously unconventional forms to clarify that his plays were subjective encounters with experience. Ibsen's deliberate concentration and reduction in *When We Dead Awaken* is analogous. However, it is important to realize that both Ibsen and Strindberg were responding to generic literary movements, emphasizing subjectivity, in their nonrealistic plays in the same way in which they were responding to convention in the realistic plays. It is equally important to realize that the multiplicity of detail, especially in the re-creation of an illusion of natural environment which realism demands, affected the development of Ibsen's language, making his imagery assume a narrower focus. In that increased specificity, each individual image informed the larger metaphoric structure more richly, giving this inner structure a greater density and scope. As well, the formal structure of the plays—that apparent cohesiveness which as Lukács notes, leads us to apply the adjective "classic" to the plays—holds our attention in a particular way, demanding that we work through the complications and obscurities in order to re-create in our response the same cohesiveness by understanding that structure and the ways in which the individual part relates to the whole. The ability of Ibsen's realistic structures to provide a deeply subjective experience tells us something, I think, about the failure of expressionism. There is no single expressionist play which we can identify as the masterpiece of the movement and respond to in the theater as an independently significant experience. Expressionism attempts to stimulate the spectator's response in the exploration of basic psychic experiences; and, consequently, the characters are blatantly archetypal. Frequently, the direct exposure of these archetypes does provoke an immediate response; but infrequently is that response profound and densely personal. Because, I think, insufficient detail is fed into the images which should stimulate, there is not enough material for our imaginations to consider and re-form into personal experience. The expressionistic second act of O'Casey's *The Silver Tassie*, for example, is much more probing an experience than most works of German expressionism and its imitations in O'Neill, because the realistic ground of the first act gives us a detailed base on which to build. The images which are blatantly exposed in the unrealistic form of the second act have content for us, and the original and unrealistic juxtaposition of them has meaning to us because of that content.

Ibsen's plays, as well, begin with an identifiable ground of reality in which certain images develop a highly complex content, and while the realistic base dissolves, it has served its purpose by feeding detail into those images which then can cease to function realistically.

Ibsen's plays resolve with no identifiable ground of reality which is fixed and certain between playwright and spectator other than the existence of consciousness itself. Reality seen as phenomena is an incomprehensible flux; reality seen mythically is an illusory vision. The plays from Ibsen's middle realistic period use the conventions of external realism to explore the essential drama of consciousness. Their popularity and the popularity of their superficial imitations have misled us. The realistic form of these plays is just that, a form, an external structure in which Ibsen could work out the processes of the mind with which he was dealing through the resolution of certain metaphors. His use of the realistic form is obviously ambiguous since while these plays seem to assume a realistic base of experience which can be examined scientifically, the endings of the plays deny that possibility. The development of realistic literature at the close of the nineteenth century was an extremely complex phenomenon. Such literature adopted the attitudes of natural science and philosophy and addressed itself to the study of environment and human nature, attempting to find new principles of behavior in a world which was the manifestation of natural processes and not the expression of divine will. However, despite the increasing awareness of the complexity and even incomprehensibility of experience, realism based itself upon the reactionary assumption that the actual nature of human experience could be understood and reproduced in art. The basis of realism is the concept of a world which can be understood. Erich Auerbach discusses the uneasy position of realism at the end of the nineteenth century and the beginning of the twentieth as the final movement of a literature grounded in a clear reality. Although he does not apply this generalization to Ibsen, the relevance of his point is clear:

As recently as the nineteenth century, and even at the beginning of the twentieth, so much clearly formulable and recognized community of thought and feeling remained in those countries that a writer engaged in representing reality had reliable criteria at hand by which to organize it. At least, within the range of contemporary movements, he could discern certain specific trends; he could delimit opposing attitudes and ways of life with a certain degree of clarity. To be sure, this had long since begun to grow increasingly difficult. Flaubert . . . already suffered from the lack of valid foundations for his work; and the subsequent increasing predilection for ruthlessly subjectivistic perspectives is another symptom.[4]

The disintegration of the central criteria and categories on which to base realistic structures to which Auerbach points is evident in the earliest moments of the development of realistic drama in the nineteenth century, at least in the work of the major playwrights. Throughout its development realism is an ambiguous dramatic form. Realism attempts to confront the nature of experience directly, but those honest confrontations encompass the incomprehensibility of that experience; the realistic work seems to assume that it is possible to represent or imitate reality accurately at the same time as it faces the obscurity of its subject.

Even in the work of Hebbel, Büchner, and Musset— three playwrights whose work is thought to signal the development of realism in modern drama—the concept of a shifting, transitional, chaotic human condition is strong. Woyzeck has become one of the most significant examples of the passive hero whose experience is determined by an equivocal reality. The various bases on which he operates dissolve for him. He suffers the attack of a nature and a society which he could never comprehend, and his victimization has become the prototype of suffering in modern drama. *Maria Magdalena* concerns a society in transition, but Hebbel's vision of change is so aggressively destructive that shifting social values destroy the younger generation and leave the father in a state of ignorance, unable to comprehend his painful experience and his participation in the events which have killed his children. In Musset's *No Trifling with Love*, the two lovers play a game of court-ship, acceptance and denial, reacting against the ex-ternal demand imposed upon them to be lovers. They recognize that their game is not reality, and the denial and suffering they enact are not painful to them because it is a game or a dance; and yet the young peasant girl cannot separate game from reality, and she kills herself when she realizes that the game is unreal. The reality of that death destroys both the game of the lovers and the real love it imitated. The subtle transitions in Mus-set between game and reality is a comic-ironic anticipa-tion of much of the explorations of the tension between the real and the illusory in modern drama.

It is interesting that realism as a serious dramatic form was extremely short lived. Auerbach's statement points to the source of its disintegration. Ibsen, Strind-berg, and Hauptmann all explored the possibilities of realism; and because of their inability to accept the fal-lacy of a consistent base of reality, moved away from realism into a more subjective drama which based itself upon the concept of an equivocal and incomprehensi-ble reality. Unable to contain the complexity of reality within the restrictions of realism, they dramatized the only reality they could formalize—the subjective work-ings of consciousness. The other great "realist" in nine-teenth-century drama, Anton Chekov, wrote within a form which gave the external appearance of realism, but his plays insist that the characters which comprise his lonely and disabled communities are each imprisoned in a private and painful isolation—that each is unable to share the reality of the other. There is neither inter-action nor communication in Chekov's dramas—only the pathetic collision of private mythologies.

Realism for Ibsen was a formal container which gave

him the freedom to explore the relationship of the self and its concept of environment with some kind of artistic discipline. However, the work of the plays destroys that formal container, dissolving the assumption that reality can be fixed and understood. Unfortunately, most of Ibsen's imitators have been influenced by the formal container and not the subjective work of the dramas themselves. However, the influence of Ibsen the realist is largely within popular drama. No major playwright, with the possible exception of the later O'Neill, has worked within the tradition of Ibsen's realistic plays. Shaw's imitations were imitations of such a subjective conception of Ibsen that they do not count. Imitations of Ibsen's realism abound in amazing proliferation, but, for the most part, these reworkings are secondary—either popular dramas filling normal emotional needs in an escapist commercial theater, or pretentious social dramas, like those of Arthur Miller, which are admirable in intent and ordinary in realization.

When We Dead Awaken is certainly a nonrealistic play, and yet its form is clearly the extension of Ibsen's use of the form of realism. The density of the environment of the realistic plays comes from Ibsen's concentration of detail, the close and detailed exploration of a smaller space into which the large spatial metaphors of the "seething abyss" and the "infinite arch" were compressed. In *When We Dead Awaken*, the concentration remains (although the actual scene encompasses a real valley and a real height) but the verbal and pictorial density is given up. The details of the landscape are reduced to a bare minimum—each resonant and yet abstracted. Part of what is abandoned is the need to give each metaphor a rational, psychological plausibility. It is as if Rubek's life consisted of nothing else other than his experience with Irene and Maja and Ulfheim; the breadth of the world is reduced to this strange and yet typical group of four figures. Each object—the champagne, the food fed to the animals, the knife, the meta-

phoric key; each conversation; each aspect of the scene
—the spa, the forest, the heights, the children playing,
inform the tension between the mythical and the phenomenal directly. The whole of Ibsen's dramas of consciousness is contained in the simplicity of this play.
Earlier I made the statement that *Brand, Emperor and
Galilean,* and *Peer Gynt* were more simple than the realistic plays; the simplicity of *When We Dead Awaken* is
quite different. In these earlier, more open plays the
simplicity derives from the expansion; the particular
concerns are more generalized—in the scope and diffu-
sion of the image of empire in *Emperor and Galilean,*
for example. In this generalization their concerns remain more vague and tentative. In *When We Dead
Awaken* the particular concerns are compressed into a reduced number of images which develop with complexity
but which allow the reader to focus upon their presence
and strategy.

The world of *When We Dead Awaken* is very small;
it contains some sense of the immediate area, the fjord,
the valley, the forests, the mountains above the forest.
The Lake of Taunitz is remembered, and there is some
vague sense of a world beyond which brings Rubek ac-
claim and which contains the museums which hold
"The Resurrection Day." But the reduced world of the
play is the only one which has any significance. Rubek
and Maja discuss their arrival in a description which
illustrates the degree of abstraction in Ibsen's development of the environment of this play:

> I noticed how silent it became at all the little road-
> side stations. I heard the silence . . . and that as-
> sured me that we had crossed the frontier—that we
> were really at home. The train stopped at all the
> little stations—although there was nothing doing at
> all . . . but all the same the train stopped for a long,
> endless time. And at every station I could hear that
> there were two railway men walking up and down the
> platform—one with a lantern in his hand—and they

said things to each other in the night, muffled, and dull, and meaningless.

This is the quality of the external world of *When We Dead Awaken*, a limbo or void in which actions, words, or gestures which may have had some former content are enacted. The only meaning which is to be wrought out of it is the experience of these four people. The scene is the phenomenal ground of their experience, and that ground is alien, hostile, and apparently meaningless. Rubek's sense of his experience is projected in that description of the journey "home" as an inconsequential, pointless series of waits at stations—places in which people enact scenes of relation and communication and significance where none exists.

The most complete extension to date of Ibsen's use of a self-defined scenic metaphor as the complete environment of the play is the scene of Beckett's plays. In these plays the nature of the self is disclosed by its relationship to its phenomenal environment, and that world is reduced to a few crucial elements—an almost barren landscape or an almost empty room. Despite that reduction, the substance of experience itself is projected in the relationships between these figures and the objects and places they use. As in Ibsen's, the content in Beckett's drama is a tension between two primary strategies of consciousness—that movement which seeks to retain identity in a ritualistic, formal use of objects and patterns of behavior external to the self, and at the same time desires a complete renunciation, a denial of the phenomenal, a giving up of consciousness itself—the "peace" or "wilderness" for which Winnie longs and fears.

Beckett shares an unresolvable paradox with Ibsen: the inability of the self to accept the mythical as the real and the inability of the self to apprehend the real without the form of the myth. For both playwrights, the paradox results in the strange transformation of basic metaphors. In the resolution of each of Ibsen's major plays the primary image of form dissolves into an image of formlessness: the Ice Church becomes the avalanche, the "infinite arch of heaven" in which silence became sound becomes alive with the dead martyred children demanding vengeance and sacrifice; the image of freedom and sanctuary traps and kills Hedvig; Rebekka, the source of light and freedom and innocence, lures Rosmer into the rushing water of the mill-race.

There is, however, an interesting difference between the relationship between external form and actual content in the plays of Ibsen and Beckett. The strict formalism of Ibsen's realism is an ordered structure whose cohesive framework we can identify and hold in mind during the course of the play, and this affirmation of order in some way protects us from the basic recognition of the plays; at least it provides us with a base which is secure enough to support us while the work of the play gradually destroys it. Beckett's plays are as strictly formal, but one aspect of their form is their insistence upon their artifice; they identify themselves as play, as formal games, arguing in some sense, against the movement of the plays emotionally. In both cases, however, the formal structure attempts to distance us (although not completely) from the despairing recognition of the play.

Ibsen's conscious formal development was an attempt to free his plays of restrictive and artificial conventions; his obvious effort was the dissolution of all which would stand between the experience of the play and the spectator's response. The convention of the box set with its sense of a complete and self-contained environment exposing its fourth wall to the spectator's imagination is built upon a concept of emotional intimacy between the plays as a whole and the consciousness of the spectator. That form of drama attempts to isolate the event of the play in a specific and private relationship between the play and the spectator, consciously ignoring, as far as possible, the artificiality of that event as it occurs within the actual theater. Ibsen never played upon the artifice of the work after his fanciful use of theatrical and formal metaphors in *Peer Gynt* in which he uses the theatrical as a conscious rhetorical device and exploits certain comic and romantic conventions. He worked consistently after that play to create private and exclusive worlds which did not bear obvious relationship to dramatic or theatrical conventions. These private and self-contained worlds, as we have seen, deal with his basic drama of consciousness. They provide a phenomenal ground in which the individual consciousness can explore its function. The use of this metaphoric environment as such a private phenomenal ground is precisely the technique of Samuel Beckett. It is far more significant that Ibsen is the precursor of Beckett's subjective drama than that he is "the father" of the patent objectivity of realistic popular drama which follows his formal structure only externally.

Beckett, of course, is able to use the metaphor of the stage and the play in his dramas of consciousness. While his environments are self-contained and insistently private, he clarifies that they are artificial worlds set up upon an actual stage. Beckett writes in a time when, as I have said before, a realistic structure would distance the spectator more than an obviously artificial one because the realistic perspective would be dismissed as inadequate to contain a profound response to experience. Beckett writes within a conventional demand that the work of art be *real*, that is, that the work of art identify itself authentically as a work of art, not as the duplication of an experience which occurred someplace else. In the late nineteenth century, as Auerbach comments, it was possible to create the illusion that there was an identifiable ground of reality which the spectator and the playwright could share. Ibsen's plays do begin upon that illusory ground, but their content works to destroy it.

Notes

Introduction

1. The major works between *Catiline* and *The Pretenders* are: *The Warrior's Barrow* (1850), *The Ptarmigan in Justedal* (1850), *Midsummer's Eve* (1853), *Lady Inger of Ostrat* (1854), *The Feast at Solhaug* (1855), *Olaf Liljekrans* (1856), *The Warriors of Helgeland* (1857), *Svanhild* (1859) revised as *Love's Comedy* (1862).

2. See, for example, Brian Downs, *Ibsen: The Intellectual Background* (Cambridge, 1948) which is an excellent study in terms of the analysis of the ideological content of the plays and the ways in which the dramas reflect that context. Brian Johnston calls for an analysis of Ibsen's metaphoric structure, a new textual criticism, but his own metaphoric analysis is used primarily to relate Ibsen to Hegel. See "The Metaphoric Structure of *The Wild Duck*," *Contemporary Approaches to Ibsen*, Ibsen Yearbook, 8 (Oslo, 1965–66), 72–95 and "The Mythic Foundation of Ibsen's Realism," *Comparative Drama*, 3 (Spring, 1969), 27–41.

3. See, for example, Muriel Bradbrook, *Ibsen, The Norwegian* (London, 1948); P. F. D. Tennant, *Ibsen's Dramatic Technique* (Cambridge, 1948); Eric Bentley, *The Playwright as Thinker* (New York, 1948); James Walter McFarlane, *Ibsen and the Temper of Norwegian Literature* (London, 1960); Brian Downs, *A Study of Six Plays by Ibsen* (Cambridge, 1950); and John Northam, *Ibsen's Dramatic Method: A Study of the Prose Dramas* (London, 1953).

4. Samuel Beckett, *Endgame* (New York, 1958), p. 44.

5. Henrik Ibsen, *Keiser og Galilæer*, *Ibsens Samlede Verker* (en Fakel-Bok), (Oslo, 1962), 2: 336, passage trans. Charles R. Lyons. All further citations from Ibsen are taken

from volumes 2 and 3 of *Ibsens Samlede Verker* and are my translations.

6. J. Hillis Miller, *The Disappearance of God* (Cambridge, Mass., 1963).

7. Martin Foss, *Symbol and Metaphor in Human Experience* (Princeton, 1949) p. 62.

8. *Bertolt Brecht: The Despair and the Polemic,* with a preface by Harry T. Moore (Carbondale, Ill., 1968).

1—Brand

1. Brian Downs, *A Study of Six Plays by Ibsen* (Cambridge, 1950), p. 58.

4—The Wild Duck

1. *Ibsen: Letters and Speeches,* ed. Evert Sprinchorn (New York, 1964), p. 237.

2. Brian Johnston, "The Metaphoric Structure of *The Wild Duck,*" *Contemporary Approaches to Ibsen* (Oslo, 1965–66), pp. 79–80, 83.

6—The Master Builder

1. *Ibsen: Letters and Speeches,* ed. Evert Sprinchorn (New York, 1964), pp. 342–43.

2. James Kerans, "Kindermord and Will in Little Eyolf," *Modern Drama: Essays in Criticism,* ed. Travis Bogard and William I. Oliver (New York, 1965), pp. 192–208.

8—Recapitulation

1. Georg Lukács, *Studies in European Realism* (New York, 1964), p. 6.

2. Lukács, p. 7.

3. Lukács, p. 131.

4. Erich Auerbach, *Mimesis: The Representation of Reality in Western Literature,* trans. Willard Trask (Garden City, 1953), pp. 486–87.

Index

Abstraction, formal: in *When We Dead Awaken*, xxix, 137

Abyss: as metaphor, xiii, xix, xviii, xx, xxi, xxvii, 2, 3, 8, 12, 16, 17, 24, 27, 32, 40, 44, 52, 59, 60, 62–63, 64, 76, 84, 90, 95, 96, 97, 98, 115, 121, 146, 151, 157, 163, 176. *See also* Antithesis; Millrace

Action: in Ibsen's plays, xxiii, 139, 166–67; in *Brand*, 2; in *Emperor and Galilean*, 71; in *Ghosts*, 78; in *The Wild Duck*, 91, 97; in *Rosmersholm*, 105, 117; in *When We Dead Awaken*, 150; in realistic plays, 159–60. *See also* Structure, dramatic

Agathon: and Julian, 54–55, 71–72; mentioned, 55, 59, 71–72

Agnes: and Einar, 3, 4; and Brand, 6, 9, 15, 35, 111; and Alf, 7, 17, 19; as Phantom, 19–21, 22; compared to Beate, Aline, and Irene, 141; compared to Rebekka, 158; and Alf and Brand, 166; mentioned, 6, 12, 13, 15, 92, 142, 156, 159

Alf: and Agnes, 7, 17, 19; and Brand, 10, 106; compared to Hedvig, 106, 159; and Agnes and Brand, 166; mentioned 12, 13, 15, 18, 79, 159

Allmers: Rita, 92; Asta and Rita, 120; Alfred, 133

Alving: Mrs. and Regina, 78; Mrs. and Oswald, 78, 79; Mrs., 78, 79, 80; Captain, 78, 169

Anitra, 37–39

Antithesis, Ibsen's use of paired concepts: discussed, xv, xxi–xxii

—ascetic vs. erotic, 19, 31, 62, 87, 92, 105, 116, 144–45

—form vs. formlessness, xvii, 51, 72, 79, 101–2, 135, 178

—guilt vs. innocence, xx, 16, 34, 76, 107, 138, 153, 161, 168

—heights vs. depths, xvi–xvii, 24, 26, 58, 64, 85, 96–97, 117, 135, 154, 175

—light vs. dark, xv, 3, 10, 54, 56, 78, 79, 93, 102, 136, 143, 145, 152

—mythical vs. phenomenal, xix, 34, 41, 52, 85–86, 100, 116, 135, 147, 161, 166, 176

—restriction vs. freedom, xv, 16, 79, 102, 154

DATE DUE